Building Research Policies

Building Research Policies

Proceedings of a seminar on Building Research Policies,
organized by the Committee on Housing, Building and Planning of
the United Nations Economic Commission for Europe, with the
Swedish Government as host.

Gävle, Sweden, 23-27 May, 1977

Published by
PERGAMON PRESS
for the
UNITED NATIONS

U.K.	Pergamon Press Ltd., Headington Hill Hall, Oxford OX3 0BW, England
U.S.A.	Pergamon Press Inc., Maxwell House, Fairview Park, Elmsford, New York 10523, U.S.A.
CANADA	Pergamon of Canada Ltd., 75 The East Mall, Toronto, Ontario, Canada
AUSTRALIA	Pergamon Press (Aust.) Pty. Ltd., 19a Boundary Street, Rushcutters Bay, N.S.W. 2011, Australia
FRANCE	Pergamon Press SARL, 24 rue des Ecoles, 75240 Paris, Cedex 05, France
FEDERAL REPUBLIC OF GERMANY	Pergamon Press GmbH, 6242 Kronberg-Taunus, Pferdstrasse 1, Federal Republic of Germany

First edition 1978

British Library Cataloguing in Publication Data

Seminar on Building Research Policies,
Gavle, 1977
Building research policies.
1. Building research — Congresses
I. Title II. Economic Commission for
Europe Committee on Housing, Building and
Planning.
690'.07'2   TH5   77-30340
ISBN 0-08-022391-5

In order to make this volume available as economically and as rapidly as possible the authors' typescripts have been reproduced in their original forms. This method unfortunately has its typographical limitations but it is hoped that they in no way distract the reader.

Printed in Great Britain by Page Bros (Norwich) Ltd, Norwich and London.

CONTENTS

Introduction   vii

Conclusions and recommendations   ix

List of rapporteurs   xix

Goals and priorities, by *F. Bertière*   1

Organization, staffing and financing (Part I): Relevance and
sponsorship of building research, by *O. Eriksson*   11

    Annex: Building Research Policies   21

Organization, staffing and financing (Part II): Organizational
structure and manpower resources of building research,
by *G. Kunszt*   25

Dissemination of information and utilization of research results
(Part I) by *V. G. Lastotchkin*   37

Dissemination of information and utilization of research results
(PartII) by *D. A. Senior*   41

    Annex   51

International collaboration (Part I): activities of the International Council for Building Research, Studies and
Documentation, by *J. B. Dick*   55

International Collaboration (Part II): review of existing
arrangements, by the *ECE Secretariat*   69

    Annex I: Key to abbreviations   80

    Annex II: Activities of non-governmental international
    organizations concerned with building research and
    development work   82

Appendix: Response papers   89

Goals and priorities   91

   Finland   91

   The National Housing Board of Finland   93

   The German Democratic Republic   95

   The Federal Republic of Germany   103

   Hungary (Technological forecast of the Hungarian building   107
   industry up to 2000)

   Hungary (System of priority programmes in building research)   111

   Netherlands   115

   Sweden   119

   The United Kingdom   123

Organization, staffing and financing   127

   Finland   127

   The German Democratic Republic   131

   The Federal Republic of Germany   137

   International Council for Building Research, Studies and   139
   Documentation (Building research policies and sponsorship
   of research)

   Netherlands   141

   Sweden   143

Dissemination of information and utilization of research results   149

   The Federal Republic of Germany   149

   Netherlands   153

   Sweden   155

International collaboration   165

   The Federal Republic of Germany   165

   Netherlands   169

INTRODUCTION

Public support for building research and development in European countries did not assume any appreciable importance until after the Second World War. In the immediate post-war years, building research was mainly concerned with technical development, but during the nineteen-fifties and sixties, functional studies were introduced both on the level of the building and of the built settlement. More attention was also paid to technico-economic problems. A principal aim of research and development was to make it possible to attain high quantitative targets of production, particularly in the housing sector.

The character of social needs has changed to some extent in the nineteen-seventies. There is more emphasis today on quality, on a better environment, on increasing the influence of the public in decision-making processes, and on the conservation of resources, including energy. There has been a marked shift of interest from problems related to the production of new buildings to those arising from the use of the existing building stock, its management and maintenance, its modernization or adaptation to new needs.

These changes have strongly influenced the directions of building research and development work, and the methods and means of organizing and financing such activities.

The re-orientation of research and development work towards new goals, or changes in emphasis from one type of research to another, must encounter resistance; it is not easy to adapt the available resources either in terms of research staff or of technical facilities. Change is needed in the educational systems associated with building research and development and much training and re-training of research workers is required. There is also an urgent need to ensure that the results of research and development work are applied in practice, by effective dissemination of information in suitable forms.

The Working Party on the Building Industry, a subsidiary body of the Committee on Housing, Building and Planning of the United Nations Economic Commission for Europe (ECE) decided in 1975 to organize a seminar which would examine in detail the problems relating to research and development in the building field.

The main aim of the seminar, it was decided, would be to discuss the various ways and means of planning, organizing, coordinating and financing building research and development activities on the national level, taking into account both the short- and long-term needs of society. While the main emphasis would be placed on governmental measures to support research activities carried out by universities, research organizations and independent experts, the steps taken to help research and development in the building materials and construction industries, for example by fiscal action or aid to education and training activities, would also be taken into consideration. The promotion of the use of research and development findings both nationally and internationally, and the methods by which international collaboration might stimulate research and development within countries and make it more efficient, would also be given attention.

ECE initiated the establishment of the International Council for Building Research, Studies and Documentation (CIB) some 25 years ago. The seminar offered a good occasion to review the results of the creation of CIB and the activities of many other organizations dealing with particular aspects of building research which could contribute to the ECE programme for the harmonization of the technical content of building regulations.

The seminar discussed policies for research and development work in the field of building materials, components and construction, but it would not take up problems and policies related to urban and regional planning research, or sociological research, which were dealt with by other subsidiary bodies of the ECE Committee on Housing, Building and Planning.

The Seminar on Building Research Policies was held at Gävle, about 200 kilometres north of Stockholm, from 23 to 27 May, 1977. Some 100 participants, representing 18 countries and 10 inter-governmental and international non-governmental organizations were welcomed by Mrs. E. Olsson, Minister of Housing and Physical Planning, on behalf of the Government of Sweden, as the host authority. They elected Gustav Cederwall of Sweden as chairman of the seminar, and Dimitri Katanov of the USSR and Arthur Newburg of the United States as vice-chairmen. The seminar was followed by a study tour in the Stockholm area from 27 to 29 May.

CONCLUSIONS AND RECOMMENDATIONS

Objectives and Priorities

Building research is a very complex activity, both because of the diversity of the objects of research, the great number of the disciplines used and the different levels of intervention at which research takes place.

Building research is important because buildings are important. Buildings are one of the major instruments of human welfare and business enterprise. They represent the largest single financial investment of most families and some businesses; they use a significantly large fraction of the world's material and energy resources; they last a long time; and we spend most of our lives in them.

Building research utilises our accumulated technical knowledge and our best technical foresight to improve building performance; to make buildings less costly to own; to make them safer to build and safer to live in; to build and use them with less waste of resources and less pollution of the environment; and to improve the quality of our private and public lives.

Building research deserves more encouragement and financial support from the governments and private institutions of the world.

It is a great responsibility to choose whose problems and what problems are to be studied and enlightened. The distribution of wealth and the standard of our habitat is very inequitable in a global, but also in a regional and national perspective. There is an urgent need for an improvement of the living conditions for the many with priority to the most deprived. An increasing part of research work in all ECE member countries should therefore be devoted to problems which are particular to the developing countries whose needs are tremendous and which have a pressing need for original solutions and methods.

Building research should be understood as the improvement of the entire knowledge required for the design and construction of buildings, i.e.:

- knowledge of man and his needs;
- data on exterior actions influencing buildings;
- sciences related to the design of buildings;
- sciences related to the construction of buildings and to construction technology.

Special attention should be paid to problems related to the maintenance and utilization of buildings, and to the people using and producing the buildings. Research in this area should include the improvement of working conditions, safety and health, and the increase of the interest of the tasts of the building workers so as to improve the conditions of their daily work.

Because of the number of the fields studied, their complexity and wide differences, there is a great number of disciplines involved, from exact sciences to experimental sciences and human sciences, including medicine and economics. At the same time these sciences must be applied simultaneously to one research subject: this requires the training of multi-disciplinary teams and, in particular, of persons capable of leading and animating their work and coordinating the intervention of different specialists.

Due to the essential difference between these various sciences as far as methods and language are concerned, there is still a gap between technical sciences and human sciences. Therefore it is necessary to give more importance to human sciences: this evolution is interesting and should be further encouraged because its object is vital.

The potential users of the research results expect a great deal of this research. Consequently they may be disappointed if they are given results which are difficult to interpret, to generalize and to apply. Research workers, particularly in the field of human sciences, must understand the very great importance of presenting their results in such a way that they can be taken into account according to their real value and will not remain unknown.

From the complexity of building research - which is apparent in its fields and disciplines - follows a great variety of levels of intervention.

These are, on the one hand, development which permits putting into practice the results of research on prototypes and testing to establish how they can be adapted to industrial production and, on the other hand, the full scale experimentation which permits testing in a reduced operation a new idea before applying it on a larger scale. The last phase is the assimilation of the research results to regulations, standardization and technical agreements. This procedure is both an effective means of disseminating research results and a support for research work of a highly applied and generally highly profitable nature.

It is essential to consider how invention can be stimulated. There are different ways of going about this, but it can be done especially by developing a policy for the training of scientists and disseminating very widely the research results in an effective and accessible manner.

Taking into account the complexity of building research, the financial constraints and the multiplicity of the disciplines and consequently of the research institutes concerned within each country, integrated research planning is needed. Nevertheless, it is important not to plan research in all its details; some flexibility must be preserved in the system.

As a preparatory stage in planning building research, future studies and technological forecasts, their international comparison and summarization should be promoted in all aspects of building and construction activities.

In a systematic way but close to the reality of facts, three hierarchical levels of objectives may be roughly distinguished:

  - the general objectives of the community;

  - more specific objectives, forming part of the preceding objectives and
    reflected in research subjects;

- clearly defined objectives which are assigned to each research subject.

It is the interest of both the society and the research workers that the choice of the general objectives should be made in accordance with the policies of governments. These objectives correspond to three types of preoccupations:

- the economic preoccupations: "better value for money"
- the social preoccupations concerned with the quality of the buildings and the wellbeing of both the inhabitants and the building workers;
- the political responsibility to ensure that resources are available.

Certain delegations considered that these objectives, having been defined and accepted at the national level, the problem was to reflect them in research themes and topics which are understandable and applicable by the research workers.

The research subjects may be drawn from four main sources:

- from the research workers whose research work requires follow-up and who can help the state to define future developments;
- from the users, who express often their points of view in the form of dissatisfaction with their present situation;
- from the building enterprises which encounter specific problems with particular projects;
- from the State, which needs the research results to define and implement its policy and as a basis for the work of codes and standards bodies.

The State has a special responsibility for the support of research which directly serve the public interest, e.g. research on noise and pollution.

A particular aspect of the choice of priorities between the different research subjects is the evaluation of the value of these subjects. Two tendencies can be noted: one is to try to quantify as far as possible the results expected from research and the other is to prefer an essentially qualitative evaluation.

The quantitative evaluation requires the use of different methods, such as cost effectiveness ratio; it is always difficult to apply even for a posteriori evaluation. It is easier to apply, however, to research work of a technical nature or related to industrial application.

The qualitative evaluation is better adapted to research work in the field of human sciences. In this case, there is a danger that using the quantitative evaluation can even lead to rejecting everything that in itself cannot be quantified. However, the research workers in human sciences should make progress towards a greater objectivity in the presentation of their aims and results, as pointed out above.

Organization, Staffing and Financing

Relevance and Sponsorship. The State should use the financing system to make sure that research is performed in the desired areas. Most important is then to find a method to identify areas of interest. This could be done, e.g. by creating a group of experts in a board for a visionary "helicopter-type" survey or by committees working out research fields within the framework of stable groups of problems.

Problem-oriented groups should be formed. They can often be relatively small, but they should consist of persons of different disciplines, e.g. technology, sociology, economics etc. They should have rather generous terms and freedom in finding methods to solve the problems. They need to have stability, continuity and time gradually to change their field of interest. A problem to which attention must be paid is the difficulty of persuading a successful researcher to give up his established area for a much more uncertain future in a new area of research.

In many cases the researchers need to be supported by a small committee of people "with both feet in actual building practice". Moreover, the mobility of R & D staff and personnel to and from industry should be encouraged. Part of certain research projects can profitably be carried out in co-operation with experts on industrial or other practical problems, in an advisory role. A two-way exchange of results and ideas should be guaranteed. Transfer teams, set up by research organizations together with practitioners from the building industry, could be formed. A wider exchange of ideas between the building industry and other industrial branches is recommended.

Bodies responsible for financing and planning should consist of all the categories which are involved in the research process or which will be affected by the results. They should be guided by goals for the research formulated in the national research programme.

In the market economy countries, the following points should be kept in mind:

- The point of departure for a discussion on organization, staffing and financing of building research is the substantial increase in resources used for building research and development work. The possibilities of re-orienting research towards new objectives, and especially to give a stronger emphasis to multi-disciplinary and integrated research, pose difficult problems. Research should deal with the building stock as a whole and not primarily with the marginal additions made to it every year. The building sector is in the midst of - or on its way towards - a "change course" situation. Society - and consequently the building industry - is entering a new phase of development. Qualitative aspects are to some extent replacing the previous quantitative shortage problems. The management of the existing built environment is gradually becoming more and more important. The limited energy resources and the shortage of raw materials etc. all over the world today are becoming more and more noticeable.

- Building research is an extensive organization today. Important research results do not become available until considerable resources and many researchers have been involved in the new problems. In a major "change course" situation, occasional new efforts are not enough. There is a need to find suitable methods to move towards new goals. In the technological area, e.g. conservation of resources, maintenance of existing buildings, it is sufficient to re-orient researchers into new problem areas where he/

she can use his/her professional background. A much more complicated situation occurs when new research objectives touch on problems of quality.

- The State should be responsible, and have the leadership in sponsoring and directing, the overall research effort, because the built environment is an essential element of human welfare. Initiative and leadership should also fall upon the State but good results are often obtained by joint efforts between the State, private enterprises and the research organisations. How financing should be shared among these groups is to a great extent dependent on the economic system of the country.

- The overall goals of nation-wide research programmes, as defined on a governmental level, should influence derived research programmes at lower levels. By a voluntary association for co-ordination, private enterprises may substantially contribute to an increase in the total research effort in a country. Insurance is needed to cover costs that may arise in cases of failure or no result of particular research projects, especially experimental buildings.

- Since the responsibility of the State is more pronounced with regard to design than to construction, a change of course in building research primarily affects design research.

Organizational Structure and Manpower Resources

Manpower problems in building research are of crucial importance. Education, training and re-training, recruitment, adjustment and motivation, creativity, performance and career development of the research personnel are basic requirements of an adequate manpower policy.

The manpower base of building research is not always broad enough for the solution of the problems exposed by society, economy and technology. Therefore, design and construction experts and other parties concerned should be involved in the overall activity of research and innovation.

The advantage of the matrix organization of research work is the effective use of research resources in ensuring adequate coordination of efforts. Therefore, this type of organisation is in many cases most appropriate. One should be aware of the dangers of over-coordination and rigidity of the research activities in the matrix scheme.

Interdisciplinary research and systems approach are decisive features of up-to-date, complex scientific research. However, some difficulties arise in connection with these trends, e.g.:

- Difficulties in understanding and assimilating theoretical instruction, concepts and methods of different disciplines;

- Lack of a research tradition and research environment in faculties of architecture and engineering;

- A tendency to set up interdisciplinary research teams without checking first that the members have progressed far enough in their particular fields of specialization;

   - If researchers come from different institutions, the institutional manage-
     ment must accept and participate in the broadening of the traditional
     subject, which is - as a rule - against its inclinations, etc.

Matrix organization, computer-aided information and decision-making, interdisciplinary research and systems approach are tools of research management.
However, the primary factor in achieving effective research results should
always be attributed to the creativity of the researcher, creativity being a
social phenomenon which can be stimulated by effective management methods.

Efforts should be made to further internationalize training and research, inter
alia to promote wider interest in problems connected with social and technological change in the developing countries. Greater consideration must also
be given to local, cultural, economic and technical conditions. This realization should characterize educational co-operation between affluent and developing countries.

Dissemination of Information and Utilization of Research Results

The timely dissemination of information on research results aiming at their
effective and most expedient utilization is of particular importance to the
successful implementation of building research policies.

Dissemination and utilization constitute important parts of the cycle of operations in which needs for research are determined, goals are established, and
the creative activity of research workers is harnessed to produce results which
are applied to the benefit of society, leading in time and along with other
developments to the establishment of new needs, goals and so on. The importance
of dissemination is shown by the fact that it can justify an amount of effort
equal to a substantial proportion of that devoted to the relevant research.

Some of the factors which influence the way in which dissemination of the results
of building research is carried out are: the broad span of relevant scientific/
technical disciplines; the complexity of the building industry and therefore of
the relations between research and its utilization; the fact that research
results represent usually only one of many inputs to a given decision so that
a system approach is needed; the fact that frequently research results have to
be synthesised and digested before they can readily be used; and the need nevertheless for reasons of economy for results to be used as soon as possible after
their production.

Dissemination and utilization have to be considered in the broader context of
technology transfer which involves questions of the environment within which
the research results will be applied, the establishment of attitudes to innovation, the need for the receiving system to adapt to the disturbance new technology creates, and adequate motivation of the user.

The multiplicity of means of dissemination reflects the complexity of the
communication problem. Although not all are primarily vehicles for transmission
of research results, the following categories can be identified:

   - Building regulations, codes, standards and technical agréments;
   - The educational system (including "in-career" industry training);

- Publications, conferences and lectures;

- Information and advisory services, including data banks (where the initiative comes from the potential user of research results);

- Specific application services geared to carry out publicity campaigns (where the initiative comes from the research side or the sponsor of the research, not from the user);

- Development groups (mixed teams of architects, engineers and administrators) which develop jointly solutions to practical problems;

- Exhibitions of research results and their potential or proven applicability;

- Mobility of technical staff who carry information and attitudes with them as they move from one employment or type of employment to another;

Important supplementary vehicles for transmission of research results are:

- Concise annotated lists and statistical data;

- Detailed reports, submitted to governmental institutions controlling the given branch;

- Prospectuses giving information on the main results of research, their expected economic effect and the address of the institute having accomplished the research work for the interested industrial organizations;

- Recommendations concerning the design, technical calculation and testing of structures, computer programmes and other information and advice for designers.

Close co-operation between research workers and users of their results is essential at all stages, not only to help in the formulation of research needs but in order to ensure that research workers have a good appreciation of the practical problems of the user, and to break down barriers to mutual understanding. However, such co-operation is not sufficient to ensure adequate translation of results into practical terms; information experts, automatic data processing and computerised information retrieval have roles to play.

Attention should be paid to the style, language and presentation of material destined for application to ensure that it is understood and accepted.

The role and feasibility of international data banks and the national organisations which would act as intermediaries merit serious examination.

One of the most effective means of achieving application of research results is their incorporation in regulations, specifications, codes and standards, but care is needed to make sure that these represent social needs and not merely those of one section of the economy.

Information must be "tailored" to suit the user who benefits from brief digests describing the "state of the art". These should be based on application, not on research categories.

There is a growing need for information to serve the public and their representatives. This is to help users of buildings to formulate and to press their demands.

An important need is safety. Levels of safety are ultimately decided by society which has a need for information to ensure that demanded levels are realistic and economic.

There is a continuing need for education to present research results and to prepare the ground for acceptance of the benefits of research. Teachers in higher education have a role here.

There is and will remain for some time a need for active campaigns to bring about the changes in attitude which will lead to improved research application. These may be general or specific. Demonstrations of successful application combined with financial or other inducements may be required.

Benefit would flow from greater knowledge of the processes involved in techno-logy transfer. One way of achieving this is to study ex post facto the reasons for success or failure of research projects.

There should be regular international exchanges of information not only on research plans and results but also on major successful applications.

International Collaboration

Many problems in building and in building research are common to many countries. International collaboration in this field is therefore essential and should be promoted by governments as an integral and important part of their policies for building research and development work.

The main goals and objectives of building research and development work, as well as the measures and means of implementing policies in this field should continue to be the subject of attention within intergovernmental organizations, such as the ECE. The ECE Committee on Housing, Building and Planning should discuss the main long-term orientation of future research and development work and, in particular, provide guidance regarding priorities for international work by means of groups composed of representatives of authorities on building research policies and of researchers. The Committee may also consider undertaking a comparative study of financial and manpower resources devoted to building research and development work in ECE countries.

In accordance with the recommendations of the United Nations Conference on Human Settlements (HABITAT 1976), substantially increased attention should be paid by the ECE and its member countries to the special problems and research needs of developing countries. Effective links should be established between the ECE and the other regional economic commissions and also between these commissions and the CIB members in their respective regions. The CIB initiative towards provi-ding an effective framework and vehicle for increased research efforts in favour of developing countries is welcomed.

International collaboration in the field of building research and development work should be promoted at all levels. Informal contacts between research managers and between researchers in specialized fields should be encouraged. Inter-organization and inter-institute collaboration should be further developed. Much more effort than in the past should be made to launch truly international co-operative research projects. CIB should pursue its investigations of possibilities of financing co-operative research projects and ECE member countries should be invited to finance such projects by appropriations from funds already available with the institutes concerned or by special contributions. Proposals for suitable projects should be submitted by the CIB to the ECE secretariat for circulation to the Working Party on the Building Industry well in advance of its June 1978 session.

National programmes should be established with full knowledge of existing programmes in other countries. Systematic arrangements should be made, therefore, for the exchange, collation and analysis of building research programmes in ECE countries. CIB should undertake a wider exchange of research programmes between its members.

International collaboration in the field of building research and development work serves the purpose of achieving economy, efficiency and quality in the research work on the national level, but may also aim at international goals and objectives, e.g. through pre-standardization work and studies paving the way for international harmonization of the technical content of building regulations. It follows that proposals for international work may be initiated either by intergovernmental or standardization bodies or by research institutes or organizations. When the initiative for international work in building research stems from an intergovernmental organization, the members of that organization should ensure that appropriate resources are made available for the implementation of the requested work either by direct support to the research organization concerned or indirectly by ear-marking national resources for the implementation of the agreed international project.

A large number of international non-governmental organizations are presently active in the field of building research and development work. A further multiplicity of such organizations is undesirable. Further efforts should be made by the ECE and the CIB to promote co-operation and co-ordination among existing organizations, so as to avoid, as far as possible, undesirable overlap in international work. Governments and intergovernmental organizations should also actively promote a rationalization of the present system of international organizations in this field by selected support to organizations of recognized repute. The CIB should strengthen its role as the principal focal point for information on international building research activities carried out by the main existing organizations in this field.

International organizations play an important role as initiators and catalysts. The services of their secretariats are required to ensure effective exchange of research programmes and results, for back-stopping of executive boards and working commissions and to assist in the organization and implementation of co-operative research projects. Measures should be taken both by governments and by the research institutes and bodies concerned to ensure that an adequate share of available resources is allocated to support the international organizations and their secretariats active in the field of building research and development work.

LIST OF RAPPORTEURS

Mr. F. Bertière, Responsable "Cellule recherche et recherche-développement",
   Direction du Bâtiment et des Travaux Publics, Ministère de l'Equipement,
   34 rue de la Fédération, 75015 Paris, France

Mr. J.B. Dick, President CIB, Building Research Establishment, Building Research
   Station, Bucknalls Lane, Garston, Watford WD2 7JR, England

Environment and Human Settlements Division, Economic Commission for Europe,
   Palais des Nations, CH-1211 Geneva 10, Switzerland

Mr. O. Eriksson, Director, National Council for Building Research, Fack
   (Atlasmuren 1), Stockholm, Sweden

Mr. G. Kunszt, Deputy Director, Hungarian Institute for Building Science,
   David Ferenc u.6, Budapest XI, Hungary

Mr. V.G. Lastotchkin, Deputy Chairman of Gosstroy of the Byelorussian SSR,
   Lenin Square 9, Minsk, Byelorussian SSR

Mr. D.A. Senior, Deputy Chief Scientific Officer, Department of the Environment,
   2 Marsham Street, London SWP 3EB, England

GOALS AND PRIORITIES

F. Bertière (rapporteur), France

DEFINITION AND DELIMITATION OF BUILDING RESEARCH

The Areas Studied

For many disciplines, the question of their purpose does not arise, since the answer is obvious and clear to all. This is not so, however, in the case of building, sufficient proof of this being provided by the variety of interpretations given to this activity by different countries, or the changing interpretations of it by a given country.

Housing was long the only form of building studied in many countries, because of its social significance and the role very often played by the public authorities in housing construction. In France, the "Plan Construction", which is an important agency for co-ordination of building research, is still concerned with housing only.

However, buildings have different characteristics according to the use for which they are intended and should therefore be studied individually. Research programmes are now, in fact, tending to take into account the problem of buildings used for other human activities, e.g. schools, hospitals, commercial premises, offices, factories and industrial buildings, etc.

Structures such as roads and distribution networks of various kinds, open air car parks, etc., which, although not buildings, form the immediate environment of buildings, may be added to this list.

A further area of research has developed more recently in some countries. It concerns the areas outside buildings, namely gardens, paving, street furniture and all the components which form the amenities of public areas and whose importance in improving life and the urban environment have been somewhat disregarded in certain building operations.

Research therefore covers all these various items and has been concerned in the first place with the way in which they are produced, including the design and execution of buildings, following a process extending from the materials, through semi-finished products and building components, to the construction itself.

The design phase calls for three main kinds of research:

- Research on design methods;

- Research on the stresses to which buildings will be subjected by the external environment;

- Research on the physical phenomena which affect buildings and permit predetermination of their reaction to these stresses.

1

Research on design methods concentrates on ways and means of generally improving and simplifying building design, e.g. functional analysis and automatic design methods.

The purpose of research on stress is to ascertain the forces which the buildings will have to withstand. Studies on wind effects, earthquakes and building load statistics are examples of research areas which may require complicated theoretical studies and extremely elaborate experiments.

Once the external stresses have been determined, determination of the building dimensions calls for a knowledge of the physical phenomena which occur within structures that are complex physical systems; research is carried out, for example, on the transfer of heat and water vapour through partitions, the transmission of acoustical vibration in buildings, etc.

The actual building process provides very important fields for research:

- Building materials; the extraction and processing of aggregates; hydraulic binder industry; adaptation of other materials for building purposes (metal, synthetics, etc.);

- Semi-finished products and building elements (terra cotta, precast concrete blocks, gypsum slabs and tiles, piping, systems for the transmission of fluids and energy, etc.);

- Building components. The industrialization of construction has given rise to substantial research programmes in many countries. Large industrially produced fabric elements, installation components, and even three-dimensional cells in concrete have been the subject of much investigation. The development of complete industrialized sectional building systems, using a small range of components, which allow great freedom in the choice of building form and type is one of the most topical subjects of research in this field.

For some years, building research has no longer confined itself to the main research theme of methods of producing buildings. There has been a growing interest in questions related to the maintenance and restoration of existing buildings; this also extends to recent buildings whose operating costs must be reduced as well as older buildings which must be saved, since people have become aware of the fundamental value of this heritage.

The relevant research concentrates on methods of analysing the condition of the buildings concerned, the shortcomings in the techniques used in the past and on ways of remedying them.

Finally, the last but not least subject for building research is the people who live in and among the buildings. People expect more from a building than a roof and shelter; the needs which housing meets are in fact immense and not well understood; this is probably one of the most extensive fields for future research and one of the least explored at the present time. The failure of certain projects due to unexpected reactions to technical and architectural innovations stems from this disregard of phenomena which were not taken into account.

The sociology of the habitat is now an important area of building research. It is not, however, the only subject involving the relationship of man and building:

illnesses caused by buildings to those who inhabit them are also an important
research topic, an example being the investigation of the possible cancerogenic
effects of asbestos in certain of its applications in the building industry.   To
conclude with this human aspect of building research, mention should also be made
of study of means of ending industrial accidents in building, which is a particularly dangerous activity.

The Sciences Used

It is apparent from the foregoing that the scope for research in building is very
wide and cannot be confined to a single objective.   The situation is further
complicated by the fact that it cannot be encompassed by a single science, building being essentially multi-disciplinary in nature.   The disciplines involved
are:

- The technical sciences, either at the basic level of physics and chemistry
  (e.g. study of materials, wind effects, acoustical transmission), or at
  the more applied level (strength of materials, soil mechanics, data processing, etc.).

- The economic sciences: building or production or maintenance processes
  need to be studied in terms of economic constraints, since the capital
  outlay in the building sector is very heavy.

- The social and natural sciences which are vital to consideration of the
  relations between man and his habitat.

- Medicine, for all matters relating to the health of occupants and the
  safety of workers.

- Architecture and the rules of the art which form the design tool.

Level of Intervention

While the field is extensive and the methods of approach are many and varied,
the levels of the research undertaken also vary.

The two most commonly distinguished levels are pure research and applied research,
which has more specific objectives.

In many countries, the building research undertaken is seldom purely fundamental
or purely applied.   This is due to the previously mentioned multi-disciplinary
character of most of the subjects of research, which involve several scientific
disciplines, each science having a more or less essential role in the research
process.

However, some building research is primarily of the fundamental kind while other
research is mostly applied, the bulk of building research activity in most countries being mostly of the latter type.   Its objectives are simpler to grasp and
its consequences easier to quantify.   The fundamental research is more prospective and is concerned with longer-term preparation for the future.

Of these two categories, pure research generally accounts for from 15 to 21 per
cent and applied research for from 80 to 85 per cent of the total research
effort in the building industry.   This is true of countries as different as, for
instance, the German Democratic Republic, Romania, the United States of America

and France. In Australia, the governmental research activities constitute a
special case. It is felt there that most of the work undertaken should be for
the longer term and priority is therefore given to pure research.

The dividing line between pure and applied research often depends on the nature
of the subject studied: investigation of the phenomena and physical laws affecting buildings and of the chemistry of materials is more in the nature of pure
research, whereas research on new processes, materials and building methods is
more applied.

F.M. Lea* distinguishes three main types of work:

> General studies for the advancement of knowledge in the building sciences,
> corresponding to pure research;

> Applied studies to solve specific and very closely defined problems;

> "Subject-object" research, which frequently has technical or economic
> aspects or a very marked multidisciplinary character.

The results of the best known phases of research, pure and applied, cannot be
put into general practice in the building industry. It is necessary to pass
through an intermediate fundamental development phase. Its purpose is to establish the necessary link between research and industry, between the laboratory
and industrial production. It consists in the planning and construction of full-
scale prototypes embodying the results of research, in carrying out tests on
such prototypes, in studying and improving details of construction and in developing the most effective execution methods and processes. The development
phase may even include the preparation of technical documentation and the provision of technical assistance during the initial applications of the results of
the development process.

This development phase, which has been given particular emphasis in the paper
submitted by the Romanian delegation,** is traditional in industry and is assuming increasing importance in building. This is because of the growing complexity of research projects, which are becoming more extensive in scope (complete
industrialized sectional building systems for various applications are frequently considered) and which also require a considerable number of increasingly
detailed scientific studies. It follows that the number of persons involved is
increasing and that their collaboration can no longer be assured on the bases
of a common tradition as in the past. It is therefore essential to undertake
integrated technological development work, first of all of a research and development nature and then, at a later stage, of a more experimental kind.

To ensure that development takes place in the most effective manner possible,
co-ordination between large numbers of experts and very strict and precise programming are required. Development projects must therefore be limited in scope,
but studied in great detail. Furthermore, they are relatively costly. In
France, a ratio of 1 to 10 is often noted between the costs of preliminary

---

*F.M. Lea. The Patterns of Building Research (London, BRS, 1962) quoted in the
report by Howenstine and Newburg (HBP/WP.2/R.18).

**Document HBP/WP.2/R.56/Add.4.

research and those of the ensuing research/development.

Because of these two factors, it is necessary to develop a procedure and a special organization for the development phase. In some countries, where research is highly centralized, research centres have developed additional activities outside their **traditional** field in order to conduct and complete this phase of research. In Romania, for example, the Building Research Institute now has a small design office which deals with many questions, as well as manufacturing workshops.

Other solutions consist in associating various research centres and enterprises in a single research project. In France, a system of assistance for industrialists wishing to undertake research and development was extended six years ago to the building sector and has led to a number of positive results in the area of industrialized building. There is a "pre-development" phase in this process in which enterprises are associated with multidisciplinary research centres and laboratories, which makes for integrated technological development.

After the development phase, and immediately prior to the application, of the processes on an industrial scale, experimental building is frequently undertaken. These buildings are not strictly speaking prototypes, but are constructed with special care and subject the new processes to the conditions of an actual building site. These operations, which are on a somewhat reduced scale, make it possible to verify:

- **on-site** technical feasibility;

- any problems of execution and manpower training;

- actual building costs.

They may be used for display purposes for users and other enterprises.

When the process has reached this point, it only remains to promote large-scale industrial **application** of the results obtained from the research. This may take several forms depending on the way in which the building trade is organized but it does not form part of the research sector.

OBJECTIVES AND PRIORITIES

The scope, scientific methods and forms of research in the building industry having been defined, some consideration must be given to the objectives of this research and to the way in which research topics are selected with a view to attaining these objectives.

Three types of objective may be distinguished:

- the general objectives of the community;

- more specific objectives, forming part of the preceding objectives, and reflected in general research subjects;

- clearly defined objectives which are assigned to each research programme subject.

The Polish delegation defined three groups of problems in its document:*

- basic problems, considered to be of national importance, and subject to government supervision;

- ministerial problems, considered to be important at the ministerial level;

- problems considered to be important for particular branches.

When a research programme has to be defined under a pre-established budget, the problem arises of proceeding with as much fidelity as possible from general objectives to objects of research and determining the choices which must be made at each stage.

The General Objectives

The community's general objectives are established by the Government and are reflected either in plans covering a number of years, as in Romania, Poland and France, for example, or in legislation, as in Finland, or in Government statements as, for instance, in the Federal Republic of Germany. They may be divided into three categories:

Economic. It is necessary, first of all, to increase the productivity of building operations and therefore to reduce building costs while maintaining quality. Another concern, mentioned, inter alia, by Norway, is to ensure a **satisfactory** distribution of economic activity, both geographically and between enterprises. The Federal Republic of Germany and France also emphasize the need to strengthen their industrial potential.

Political. The main objective here is to secure greater national self-sufficiency. In most energy importing countries, this has resulted in the recent launching of many research projects aimed at saving energy in the construction and operation of buildings, or, as in Romania, for example, finding buildings methods that will make full use of national resources. A further aspect of the quest for national independence is to be found in one of the objectives of France's Plan Construction namely, encouragement of exports by French enterprises. Some countries, such as the Federal Republic of Germany, consider that one of the major objectives of their research promotion activities is the strengthening of their scientific potential.

Social. Here the concern is to achieve prosperity and increased well-being for the entire population, and in particular for the most disadvantaged. The aim of the research will be to obtain **better** quality housing, on the one hand, and healthier, safer and more comfortable conditions for building workers, on the other. A more forward looking objective, stated by France, is that of preparing the housing of tomorrow. This means anticipating the changes that will occur in society, so as to ensure the availability in the future of the building techniques needed to meet new requirements. It will be noted that these objectives are often contradictory, at least at first sight. For example, efforts to achieve greater productivity are not clearly compatible with the desire to improve working conditions in the building industry. Neither is it obvious that energy saving will, in the short term, be consistent with savings in building

---

*HBP/WP.2/R.56/Add.5.

costs. This further complicates subsequent choices, since, ideally, one should find the best possible answer to these problems as a whole, not to each one of them. A further comment, which also helps to illustrate the difficulty of defining priorities, is that many of the objectives are basically qualitative and difficult, if not impossible, to translate into quantitative terms.

Objects of Research

The general objectives established by the government must then be translated into matters for investigation by those responsible for building research. In all countries, this phase involves extensive consultations among those responsible for activities in the building sector.

These consultations are generally conducted in joint working groups on which sit representatives of research workers, users, enterprises, industrialists, officials responsible for following up research, investors in building, design office engineers, architects and university teachers. In France, the Plan Construction which brings together experts in these different professional categories, functions in this way. A working group is appointed to consider a specific question, which discussion within the Plan Construction has shown to be of prime importance. This working group avails itself of all the expert advice it deems necessary, from both within and outside the building sector. Examples of such questions are "Housing and Energy". "Housing and Health" or "External shells, partitions and cladding of buildings". The group reviews the current situation and practices in the industry and the research already carried out, identifies the points on which progress seems to be needed and, finally, proposes specific subjects for research in order to achieve this progress.

With some differences of form, this practice is general in all countries. In Poland, co-ordination units are entrusted with certain matters considered at the governmental level to have priority; in Norway, the Royal Norwegian Council for Scientific and Industrial Research (NTNF) establishes priorities by means of specialized advisory committees. In the United Kingdom, the officials who make up the membership of programme review committees interpret the needs of users, within those committees; in Sweden, all interested parties meet in the Swedish Building Research Council. There does not appear at this stage to be any really quantitative method of determining subjects for research. The definition is arrived at as a result of discussion among the various parties concerned.

Thus, the subjects may be drawn from a number of different sources:

From the research workers themselves, whose current research indicates the need for other work in the future;

From the users, who state a certain number of needs or their dissatisfaction with the housing offered to them;

From the building enterprises which encounter on-site problems whose solution frequently calls for a research effort they do not always have the means of undertaking;

From the public authorities who need the results of various research projects to be able to implement their policy and carry out their tasks.

The participation of these different sources varies from country to country. The United Kingdom delegation, for instance, considers that most projects originate from research workers themselves. It depends, in fact, on the type of research to be carried out. Because of its complexity, fundamental research is often suggested by those best able to define it, namely, the research workers.

Research of a highly applied nature is usually suggested by enterprises which are faced with particular problems. More rarely, it is proposed by users or by the public authorities.

Subject-object research, or long-term prospective research, is usually, as in France, suggested by the public authorities responsible for preparing for the future by anticipating, as far as possible, the demands which the technicians of the future will have to meet. Thus prospective research may be of great help in taking decisions that are necessary today and will determine the future. In France, the policy deemed a priority one, of so-called "open" industrialization by compatible components has been the subject of several prospective research projects intended to inform the administration regarding its current options.

The Choice of Research Subjects

The last phase in the establishment of a research programme consists in selecting the specific subjects for research within the themes, as well as the research workers who will conduct this research.

Newburg and Howenstine* point out that building research is generally considered to be very profitable. However, in many cases it is difficult to assess the profitability of a research project. This is demonstrated by two radically opposed opinions: the delegation of the German Democratic Republic holds the view that all theoretical and applied research should yield a measurable economic effect,** while the Norwegian delegation*** recognizes that there is obviously a large degree of uncertainty involved in estimating a priori the quality of the solutions which one sets out to find.

Once the objectives have been satisfactorily determined, the selection of research projects is made in many countries by consulting a number of governmental or non-governmental experts whose competence is recognized in the sector concerned. This course is followed in France, where an effort is made to have each research project assessed by several experts, in terms of a set of criteria designed to ascertain the cost effectiveness ratio of the research. However, the criteria are not weighed in a strictly mathematical fashion.

It should be noted that the selection of subjects for research and development projects, which are much closer to industrial operations, is much easier. A relatively accurate estimate can be made of the likely industrial impact of the research findings; calculation can then be made for a given period and the cost effectiveness ratio of the development undertaken may thus be determined fairly accurately. However, experience shows that considerable errors may be made in either direction in this kind of assessment.

In the case of research which has not yet reached the development stage, the systematic elimination of investigations which do not seem likely to be fairly

---

*Document HBP/WP.2/R.18.
**Document HBP/WP.2/R.56/Add.6.
***Document HBP/WP.2/R.56/Add.2.

profitable is dangerous in the long term for the sector's vitality and innovation capacity. This is because the most fruitful inventions are rarely promising
at the outset. Those in charge of research should therefore ensure that some
provision is made for longer-term research. Fundamental research is a case in
point. This type of work accounts for at least 20 per cent of the total research
effort in all countries. Some efforts are, however, being made to base the selection of research subjects on a more quantitative than qualitative study of
the consequences of the probable findings.

In several countries, and particularly in France, increasing use is being made
of value analysis as an aid in the programming of building research. A number
of experiments have shown that the value analysis originally developed for industrial products can be applied, with certain adjustments, to the building field.
It involves subdivision of a building project according to the functions it is
desired that the building should fulfil rather than according to the traditional
structural breakdown. The value of the different functions is then calculated
in the light of the needs to be met. This method of operation provides information for evaluating a research project or its aim. Preliminary research has
thus been undertaken to determine the values to be achieved for the various
functions of a building. They are then used for research project evaluation
based on the methods and techniques to be used in actual building to ensure
fulfilment of these functions.

The Romanian delegation indicates in its paper* that the Building Research
Institute (INCERC) uses a special method to assess the economic value of research
in construction. We believe it is worth drawing attention to the principles of
this method.

The principal indicators used are:

    - The coefficient of economic value Ea

$$Ea = \frac{\text{Additional benefits from the research for the duration of the economic life}}{\text{Expenditure on research + Expenditure on application of the results}}$$

    - The time taken to recover the expenditure Tr

$$Tr = \frac{\text{Total expenditure}}{\text{Average additional benefits appearing throughout the economic life}}$$

    - The net effects of the research A

$$= (\text{Total additional benefits}) - (\text{Total expenditure})$$

Values for these different indicators are estimated when the research is initiated,
determined with accuracy upon completion of the research and verified during the
application of the results.

---

*HBP/WP.2/R.56/Add.4, Annex III.

Because the information available is too fragmentary, it is not possible to analyse the way in which those effects of research which are difficult to quantify are taken into account. We are also unable to furnish comparisons between the estimated, refined and verified values of the indicators, although such comparisons would be valuable in respect of a method which seems to be highly useful.

In concluding this preliminary report on the objectives and priorities of building research, attention is drawn to two points which seem to be quite clear:

- Building research is highly complex and is becoming more so, both in its objectives and in the sciences it employs, and the procedures it uses;

- The methods used for selecting the objectives and priorities are still for the most part qualitative and subjective. There is much work to be done in this field, particularly since research projects are becoming increasingly complex.

ORGANIZATION, STAFFING AND FINANCING: (PART I)

RELEVANCE AND SPONSORSHIP OF BUILDING RESEARCH

O. Eriksson (rapporteur), Sweden

Two introductory reports are presented on each subject. This report deals with
the question of the relevance of research with the problem of keeping national
development and research in step with each other and with financing as a means
of steering. It is hoped that it, along with the other report on Subject B
(Organizational structure and manpower planning in building research), where
the emphasis is on the organization of building research as a part of national
organization and manpower planning seen from the sponsor's viewpoint, will cover
the theme from the standpoints of the different ECE member countries. For both
papers the common aspect is that the problems are mainly seen in conjunction
with a situation of change in overall goals and priorities.

ORIENTATION OF THE REPORT

Building research represents part of one, and sometimes more than one, sector
of the community. At the same time, it also forms part of the community's
scientific research complex. The ECE countries would seem to agree that sectoral roles are of decisive importance to the overall organization of building
research.

A trait common to all countries would appear to be the fact that the field of
building research covers technical and natural science research and development
on the design of buildings and in particular residential buildings, and on the
actual construction of these buildings. Given this common denominator, the
scope of building research has been extended to varying degrees and in various
directions: to other parts of the urban planning – construction – management
chain; to fields of urban development such as transport systems, water supply
and sewerage and energy distribution; to parts of the environmental protection
field and the work environment; and to disciplines other than natural sciences
and technology.

From the organizational standpoint, too, building research is a complex concept.
Building research is not planned and conducted solely by and at State-run
building research institutes, but also by the following other bodies; universities and polytechnics, institutes of technology, specialized research institutes financed by the State, institutes for individual branches financed jointly
by the State and industry; private, non-profit making institutes financed via
fees charged for work commissioned, private, co-operative and State-owned companies and, last but not least, authorities whose terms of reference include
the building sector. The statement that it should be possible to finance work
both via internal funds and via public funds allocated for research holds good
in the case of both companies and authorities.

In addition to the planning of the activities of bodies conducting research,
planning in the longer term and steering of research work takes place through
the medium of the Parliament, the Government/Ministries and public and semi-
public bodies such as Commissions, councils and academies. This responsibility
for planning is often accompanied by responsibility for financing.

11

This report concentrates on the organization and financing of building research using the responsibility of the community as a sponsor of research as a point of departure. As actual conditions vary from one ECE country to another, the report has been worded in general terms and is problem-oriented.

TWO TASKS FOR RESEARCH

Research has, in principle, two tasks to fulfil in each sector of the community. It should (a) help implement decisions and achieve goals that have been set up, and (b) help set up new goals.

The emphasis in present-day building research lies on Task (a). This has very strong sectoral ties and is part of a national organizational system, the purpose of which is to help goals materialize. It can be described as research aimed at change and development. Organization and financing are designed to promote efficiency in the research apparatus.

Task (b), to acquire new knowledge which will help set up new goals, is different in nature and makes to some extent different demands of organization and financing. Research with these aims must be geared to describe, understand and explain more than to bring about change and development. This research must incorporate critical analysis of the sector in question and the results achieved. It must be capable of dealing with problems which other bodies in the sector have not yet considered of interest. Organization and financing should be designed to establish integrity, keep a general eye on matters and be progressive.

Should then the tasks of building research be limited to being tools used in the implementation of decisions, or should this research also be responsible for Task (b), i.e. to help set up new goals ? This issue is very much akin to the discussions now taking place in many quarters on technology assessment, i.e. systematic studies of the consequences which the application of technical methods (already in existence or new) may have for the community in the long term. And there are conflicting tendencies here. The opinion seems, however, to predominate that technology assessment should be a natural ingredient of all the decision-making processes found in society which concern technical systems in a decisive manner. Technology assessment cannot, therefore, be regarded as an isolated or highly specific activity. It should be conceived in close contact with the organizational environment in which it is to be used and should be designed as a part of the normal decision-making process. This type of approach means that building research should according to both (a) and (b) be kept together by a national organization.

This conclusion, however, may not be allowed to lead to all research with a critical slant being restrained within the boundaries of the sector. Knowledge derived from outside cannot be spared. But even with a reservation such as this, the consequence will still be that the circle of persons with an interest in building research will have to be widened to include those affected by the results of construction, i.e. the entire community. Planning and financing of building research may no longer remain a task for experts. Special committees, commissions and councils with the job of planning and financing, plus the boards of research institutions responsible for their own planning must have a very varied composition representing all parties with interests in the research.

This report is based on the assumption that building research does have a wide-ranging and coherent task to fulfil and that this task is of prime importance to an extremely wide circle of persons. It is only in the light of a hypothesis

such as this that it becomes relevant to speak of a situation of change in
overall goals and priorities.

CHANGE AS A PROBLEM

Behind the present interest in technology assessment, which has manifested itself,
for example, in initiatives taken on an international scale (OECD), lies a more
subdued optimism as regards material development. The realization of the limitations of our natural resources plays a major role in this respect. Interest
in the nature and implications of growth is increasing at the expense of its
extent. Objections have also been raised as to the fact that technical changes
tend to determine developments, and not people's needs. One-sided technical
development has time and again proved to lead to the emergence of new problems.
Even among those who believe in technology, there is a growing awareness of the
fact that the direction in which we are moving needs to be reviewed.

Discussions on Subject A, Goals and Priorities, should throw a considerable amount
of light on the situation prevailing in the building construction sector as regards
viewpoints on orientation in the future. If we look back over the years, we note
that changes have constantly been taking place in parts of the sector. Developments and adjustments to the course set are nothing new, despite the fact that
the orientation has remained more or less the same. It would seem, however,
that the rate of change has now increased or is about to increase in the ECE
area and that we would therefore be justified in speaking of a major general
change of course.* In what follows, we therefore confront a "keep-on-course"
situation with a "change-course" situation. This is one way of focusing interest on change as a problem. Any account to be fitted into the framework of
a brief report obviously has to be general. There are of course parts of the
building research field which are not affected more by a "change-course" situation than by the gradual changes always in progress. This, however, need not
mean that the perspective of change is not relevant to building research in its
entirety.

"KEEP-ON-COURSE"

In a purely "keep-on-course" situation it is reasonable to assume that the entire
research organization has already achieved a high level of motivation. The goal
structure - i.e. the complex of goals which constitutes the lode-star of the
work - is well established and accepted at all levels. Changes occur in individual goals, but not so often and so rapidly as to be regarded as changes in
the entire goal structure. Not only is the research organization well developed
and adjusted to the goal structure, but the sectoral organization too. Research
becomes an integrated part in a goal-oriented system. The scope for interplay
between research and implementing bodies in the sector is highly developed. The
sectoral bodies can influence research. Furthermore, it is relatively easy for
the research community to convey their results to the proper consumers.

Generally speaking, the "keep-on-course" situation is marked by a strong capacity for "auto-piloting" within its sector. There is an almost total consensus
of opinion on the subject of goals and means and a strong measure of congruency
between problems to be solved and the organization delegated to solve them.
Corrections of course are made gradually in certain zones without necessitating
a change in the main orientation. The gaps in the knowledge available which

---

*For further information on the background in the ECE member countries see annex.

B

exist or which emerge in the course of time as a result of change within a
sector, are not as a rule so great as to prevent them from being filled by
moderate extensions of the fields of activity of the bodies responsible for
research and development.

The most outstanding example of a "keep-on-course" situation is the major orientation towards issues concerned with construction of new housing, which has long
been a feature of building research in the ECE countries. The need for tackling
the problem of providing housing has everywhere led to the creation of a strong
organizational structure in both the public and private sectors. Research has
been faced with clear goals. The circle of interested parties has been limited
and well defined, and it has therefore been a fairly simple matter to organize
channels of contact between them. The said interested parties - i.e. authorities, developers and the building industry - have possessed the qualifications
and resources necessary to be able to state their case and maintain it in the
context of research planning.

It is also easy to point out zones of building research which are clear examples
of a "keep-on-course" situation. One firmly established goal of long standing
is, for instance, that buildings shall be of sufficient strength and stability.
And indeed, research on the load-bearing structure of buildings has been in
progress for a long period of time and the problems involved are amply represented in both research and teaching circles. Requirements and loads are set
out in standards and recommendations, and research on the subject has produced
a good supply of knowledge on technical solutions. This knowledge has also been
applied in the practical context.

Research on the structural aspects of buildings is a good example of successful
research and development. It is today also an example of the problems which
arise when we begin to approach the goals. Research runs the risk of becoming
bogged down by studies of the finer details of problems, with a rapid decline
in its usefulness as a result. At the same time, the organizational apparatus
of research is strong and has the capacity to hold its own in the struggle for
new funds. This zone may therefore also serve as an example of the problems
associated with a "change-course" situation.

THE "CHANGE-COURSE" SITUATION

A "change-course" situation in the context of building research has its origins
in the fact that our society now needs to re-orient activities in the building
sector. Completely new goals are emerging for this sector, and some already
established goals are undergoing change. Others are being retained. The outcome
of the increased rate of change is a new goal structure which replaces the one
which previously served as a guide and according to which the organizational
structure in the building sector was shaped. The overall aim of research remains,
however, unchanged - namely, to produce the new knowledge necessary as a basis
for defining goals, giving them a concrete configuration in terms of decisions
and implementation of these decisions. But the need for fresh knowledge and
for knowledge of completely new fields is probably so great in a "change-course"
situation for it to be justifiable to speak of a "change-course" situation even
when it comes to research.

If we for a moment revert to the "keep-on-course" situation we see that the
strong organizational structure developed for this situation comes close to
blocking the course of progress in a situation of change.

The new impulses produced by a change in national development find difficulty
in reaching the old, well-known, goal-oriented sectoral organization. Furthermore, research, insofar as it takes up these problems, finds it difficult to
obtain support from established clients and to locate a natural consumer for
the new knowledge. Also, if these impulses first manifest themselves in other
parts of the sectoral organization, there is frequently a lack of natural links
with the research structure. In the case of problems which lie outside the
current operational framework for research, there is often a lack of both suitable research environments and qualified people. It is difficult to get research going even if resources in the form of grants were to be available.

The inherent unwieldiness of the system also means that adjustment of the organizational structure of the sector to the new situation and the new goal
structure takes place fairly slowly. The actual change-over is delayed by the
fact that the old goals set up for the sector live on throughout the transitional period. They gradually fade out, but the shadow of the past remains.
The transitional period is therefore extra complicated. But gradually, once
the new goal structure has been accepted at all levels and the organization
adjusted to it, the sector finds itself in a new "keep-on-course" situation.

A general feature of a "change-course" situation is that the sector needs strong
signals from outside. The capacity for self-steering is limited. New goals
arrive from elsewhere, generated by for instance social problems or a new view
of management of our natural resources. These win only slow acceptance in all
branches of the organizational structure. This means that there is neither a
consensus of opinion on goals and means nor congruency between problems which
need to be solved and the organization which is to solve them. Changes of
course in different zones of the sector accumulate and lead to change of the
main direction. Gaps in knowledge suddenly become so large that the existing
research and development bodies find themselves incapable of filling them by
making minor alterations to the scheme of activities. In some cases, the
stumbling block may be lack of research specialists in a subsidiary discipline,
while in others it may be that the established organizational structure does not
suit the new problems, or is not prepared to tackle them because they are regarded as irrelevant or unworthy of attention in a traditional perspective.

The oil crisis and its effects for the planning of research in general, and to
an extent building research too, is an excellent example of a "change-course"
situation. There has been no lack of voices in research circles that have already drawn attention to the scarcity of energy as a factor of significance to
the future orientation of research. Research had already been done on these
issues. However, it was only with the advent of the oil crisis and the breakthrough for energy conservation goals, plus the resulting need for alternative
sources of energy, that a real demand for this type of knowledge arose.

The nations affected reacted quickly, given an extra push by the serious economic
crisis which followed in the wake of the oil crisis, and drastic measures were
introduced. National research programmes supported by generous grants were
drawn up and co-ordinated by bodies directly subordinate to the government. In
certain cases, new bodies were set up to deal with the planning and financing
of research and development. International co-operation was promoted via government agreements, and special joint bodies with completely different potential than, for instance, the CIB working commissions, were created in a short
space of time.

For the time being, the oil crisis and energy research represent an extreme

example. It does demonstrate, however, what scarcity of resources can mean to
national development and planning of research. If the opinion that we are moving
towards a general scarcity of resources is correct, we must expect a number of
changes in course, which in the long term may prove quite significant, without
necessarily needing to have been preceded by crises. The signs of change in
course which might be discerned in the building sector itself are by and large
less dramatic. The signals are, however, noticeable for those ECE countries
which have begun to feel the effects of being close to or having already reached
the goal of eliminating the housing shortage.

It is, for instance, noticeable how the role of physical planning as part of an
integrated physical, economic and social planning is beginning to be stressed
at the expense of its role as a step preparatory to the development of virgin
land. Studies of welfare based on the "Quality of Life" concept are beginning
to replace performance studies of individual factors. Modernization is becoming
a major occupation alongside new construction, something which generates a completely new approach to the building process. Management of the existing, largely new, stock of buildings and works is assuming the guise of an increasingly
vast task which, from the research standpoint, is in its infancy – and which
possibly can be equated in importance with construction itself. In addition,
urban development techniques are assuming more and more importance parallel to
the discipline which has dominated the scene up to now – namely, building construction. Energy problems and interest in issues connected with the work environment have brought branches of engineering concerned with indoor climate to
the fore, i.e. lighting, heating and ventilation. Not even the area covered by
classical building techniques has remained untouched. Observation of the risks
to health caused by chemicals and the increasing number of persons suffering
from allergies, as well as rising maintenance and operational costs, are all
points which indicate that the focus of interest should perhaps be shifted away
from problems concerned with the structural framework of buildings towards
questions connected with surface finish, facing and cladding.

ORGANIZATION AND FINANCING

Organization and financing are both means of influencing and facilitating research and development. They are therefore dealt with together in the following
review of certain important questions.

WHO SHOULD SPONSOR, THE INTERESTED PARTIES OR THE STATE ?

There is research and development which is financed and conducted by private,
co-operative or State-run organizations. At the other end of the scale we get
research and development financed by the State and conducted by State research
bodies. In between the two extremes, there are various hybrid forms. The question is which mix of organization and financing one should choose.

Research and development should as far as possible be conducted in decentralized forms close to the problems on hand and close to the people who will use
its results. All this speaks in favour of having the parties involved with
the building sector as sponsors. However, this theory is not without its limitations. A number of questions remain.

- do the interests of the parties concerned in the building sector auto-
  matically coincide with those of the state and the users ?

- how can the interests of those lacking resources, e.g. the users, in
  research and development be taken into account ?

- how should the basic stock of knowledge be organized ? How are wide-ranging and overlapping problems to be handled ?

- how is support to be given to critical, analytical research ?

Points for Discussion:

If we sum up the answers to the questions, the conclusion will be that the State must be responsible for a substantial measure of research and development work. How much then should that be in a "change-course" situation ? Should that amount increase or decrease compared to a "keep-on-course" situation ? Should it concentrate on special issues, e.g. issues which are new, or of importance to interested parties with meagre resources etc. ?

SPONSORSHIP - BUSINESS ENTERPRISE RESEARCH AND DEVELOPMENT

The parties with an interest in the field which can act as sponsors are companies. As a rule, they have their own research and development programmes and thus the roles of research and development body and sponsor are fused into one. Business enterprise research and development has been and still is of major importance. The State therefore also has good reason for acting as sponsor for research and development carried out by companies. Research and development must offer potential for economic gains if companies are to find it interesting. One prerequisite for this is that national regulations should not place unjustified obstacles in its path. For a long time now the ECE countries have been trying to reorganize building regulations, standards and so on in a way which would release development potential latent in companies. This has produced results with both advantages and disadvantages - genuine improvements have been mixed with superficial design. There are however scarcely any definite signs of a marked increase in research and development initiated by companies.

Points for Discussion:

Need the state increase the amount of economic support given to company research and development ? What form should such support take in a "change-course" situation ? Are the impulses which steer events otherwise so strong that such support may be of a general nature (e.g. tax relief etc.) or should it be given in the form of grants for research and development projects ?

SPONSORSHIP - RESEARCH AND DEVELOPMENT AT INSTITUTES, UNIVERSITIES AND POLYTECHNICS

As far as research and development conducted at special institutes and colleges of polytechnics is concerned, the sponsorship provided by the parties with a vested interest in results is normally limited to financing of projects on a contract basis. State sponsorship, on the other hand, includes both financing and organization. The emphasis in this section is therefore on the contribution made by the State.

The way in which research and development is financed is of major importance. K. Fantl (Austrian Institute for Building Research, CIB VI Congress Papers) distinguishes between three methods.

(a) Contracts or research upon order, i.e. direct assignments given to bodies conducting research and development when the initiative and the planning comes from the financer - who in this case may also be a party with a vested interest in the work.

(b) Research upon application. The initiative may be mixed, but the programme for the work is usually drawn up by the research and development
organization which has applied for the grant.

(c) Basic financing, commonly allocated on an annual basis for the entire
research and development body. Initiatives in terms of projects and
planning are largely the responsibility of the body conducting the
research and development.

At present, Type (b) seems to be predominant. Research and development organizations in general regard Type (c) as the best. It is considered to offer
good prerequisites for planning, continuity of work, security for staff and so
on. In a "keep-on-course" situation, where there is agreement as to the goals
and where supervision by the State concentrates on the efficiency aspects, it
may prove natural to make basic financing available to experienced organizations
with qualified research and development staff and a highly developed internal
structure. The type of financing which is considered to be best will be a form
of reward after a trial period of research upon application and upon order.

Given a "keep-on-course" situation, it is wise to consider whether the same
pattern is suitable. The problem here is to redistribute resources among priority areas. This is, of course, to a certain extent done through established
research and development bodies changing their orientation. It probably also
has to take place to a certain extent through slowing down activities in the
hands of established bodies and transferring financial resources to completely
new research and development organizations. The choice of financial methods
may also be used as a means to stimulate the growth of new research and development bodies oriented towards the major gaps in knowledge.

Points for Discussion:

Is financing according to Type (a) a good method in a "change-course" situation ?
Are there limits to its usefulness, e.g. towards development work rather than
pure research ? Does Type (a) assume that established research and development
bodies exist to take on assignments ?

Should financing according to Type (c) be used in a "change-course" situation to
put a premium on interest in new problems, and on willingness to take risks with
research which may be of less value from the standpoint of internal academic
merits etc. instead of favouring "long and faithful service" etc. ? State sponsorship must also cover organization of bodies conducting research and development.

As a rule, a research set-up organized on a project by project basis is considered to offer greater flexibility than a traditional linear set-up. This type
of organization has also been tried out by the building research institutes. At
universities and polytechnics the linear set-up is strictly governed by the rules
of academic life. One of these would seem to be that new professorships are only
created when a problem has become established as a scientific discipline or sub-
discipline. This is far too slow a process in the context of a "change-course"
situation. Changes in institutional structure may not therefore be used as a
means to obtain research advancing towards practical solutions in new fields.

Under the terms of a UNESCO project entitled "International Comparative Study
of the Organization of Research Units" a preliminary report of a Swedish study
has been presented. It indicates that alongside the official complex of facul-

ties, departments and so on, there is also a more informal type of structure in
the form of research teams. Three-quarters of all those involved in scientific
and technological research belong to such teams. It may therefore be worth while
giving a brief account of the results, despite the fact that they are only preliminary as yet.

- 80 per cent of the teams constitute an independent entity within a
  department. 15 per cent consist of researchers from more than one
  department and only 5 per cent are identical to the notion of department.

- Research teams often select their own projects. On the average, the
  influence of the bodies concerned with research policy is slight, although
  it is above average in the engineering sciences.

- The majority of the teams choose their orientation according to the
  urgency of the situation in scientific terms. Teams belonging to the
  engineering sciences and geology, however, concentrate more on practical
  usefulness.

- Orientation towards practical usefulness has an inverted relationship
  to the age and experience of the head of the team.

The preliminary image created by the report is interesting. Even if teams seem
to be directed mostly from inside, they may possibly offer a means of solving
the conflict between institutionalization and a "change-course" situation at
polytechnics and universities.

Points for Discussion:

Is a direct interplay between bodies responsible for research policy/sponsors
and research teams alongside the formal organization a way of stimulating problem-oriented research ? How is the emergence of teams to deal with relevant
problems to be stimulated ? Is the scope for establishing research teams limited
by larger, more obvious gaps in the formal organizational structure ?

The special institutes represent the exact opposite of the universities and polytechnics. They have a business enterprise structure with an executive body and
permanent staff. This makes them suitable for dealing with composite problems
and for carrying on work continuously over long periods. In a "change-course"
situation, this structure may be a weak spot. Major changes in course call for
further training and also retraining of personnel - something which lies outside
the scope of this report. Different forms of matrix organisation may correspond
to the informal system of research teams found at universities. The interplay
between a research team and a policy-making body, which should be capable of
generating change in the university context, must at the special institutes take
the form of interplay between policy-making bodies and institute management and
between management and project groups.

Points for Discussion:

Can the proper organization of the institutes help make them receptive to new
problems ? Does management of the institutes play a key role in this context
and, if so, what line should it take ?

THE STATE AS A SPONSOR - BODIES RESPONSIBLE FOR FINANCING AND PLANNING

It is obvious that in a "change-course" situation, sponsorship must be of the active type, contribute to opening up new fields of problems and to implementing new or amended goals in research circles. There is therefore every reason to discuss the financing and planning level of the national research organization. It is obvious that responsibility for financing is accompanied by the ability of at least negative steering - refusal of grants. In a "change-course" situation, positive steering is, however, more important. What has to be done is to identify and describe problem fields with credibility, generate enthusiasm for research in new priority areas, recognize new, important research ideas when presented and so on.

The organization will naturally be highly dependent upon community organization in general. But questions still remain to be discussed.

Points for Discussion:

Should sponsoring bodies be closely linked to national political power ? Should they be autonomous bodies with their roots in the circle of interested parties ? Should they have specialist knowledge of the issues to be solved or specialist knowledge of matters of research ?

Finally, I have considered raising the question of financing in general via the national budget or special levies. It is difficult to establish a congruent levy for a broad range of building research in which urban planning and management are ingredients. Important interested parties, e.g. on the user side, also lack the funds with which to pay research and development levies. A levy instead of financing via the national budget will therefore be an issue with practical, fiscal connotations rather than an issue concerned with sponsorship and relevance. I therefore feel that this issue falls outside the focus of interest of this report.

ANNEX

BUILDING RESEARCH POLICIES

Relevance and Sponsorship of Building Research

Do such tendencies towards a change in development in the community as a whole exist and are we justified in the building sector in starting a discussion on the organization and financing of building research in the change perspective ?

Background in the ECE Member Countries

Building research in the ECE countries is largely concerned with the provision and construction of housing. It has direct correlations with situations and goals for national development in the ECE countries during the post-war period. Housing shortage has been a predominant feature of the scene in all countries. And everywhere a concerted effort has been made to solve the problem. The economies and national organization of the respective countries have been sufficiently strong to lend realism to the goal of eliminating the housing shortage within the foreseeable future by means of new construction. Economic resources and the capacity and manpower assets of the building industry have been limiting factors. The trend has therefore been towards an increasingly industrialized form of construction. The building of vast housing estates has favoured industrialized methods and has at the same time been part of the general structural changes taking place in society.

Naturally, we have not turned a blind eye to problems in the built environment other than those of housing shortage. Far from it. However, the gravity of the housing problem and the possibility of solving an acute national dilemma still led the focus of the building sector and thus of building research to shift towards productivity issues. The role of physical urban planning as a preparatory step towards building construction assumed a prominent place and the necessity of producing the largest possible number of dwellings for the funds available caused interest in operational costs to take a back seat. The building process ranging from underdeveloped land to occupation of dwellings was adjusted to an increasing degree to ideas borrowed from stationary industry. Quantifiable and measurable expressions were sought even for the ambitions to build quality housing. Qualitative factors which could not be measured were pushed into the background. Far more time was spent in discussing national uniform, easy to apply rules and rational decision-making than was spent on the need for giving consumers a say in planning and building. Harmonization of building regulations and standards became a means of facilitating industrialization on a large scale. Meanwhile regional and local variations in building were relegated to the background.

Development Perspectives in the ECE Countries

The result of this concentration of efforts on housing construction has been a widespread improvement both in quantitative and qualitative terms of living

21

conditions for the major population groups. Of this there can be no doubt, despite the fact that individual housing estates may be criticized for short-comings in quality in various respects. The ECE countries are now nearing the winning post - i.e. the elimination of the housing shortage - more or less on schedule. Furthermore in the countries which for various reasons have come closest to the goal or have largely reached it, it is clear that all problems are not thereby solved, and that new problems are emerging.

The fact that the existing stock of buildings - largely of recent date - repre-sents a vast reserve of cultural, social and economic resources, rising opera-tional costs and increasing interest in preservation of our cultural heritage have helped bring the question of management of that existing building stock into the limelight. Extensive alteration and modernization of the older stock of buildings is taking place and this is promoting an entirely new view of the building process. Physical planning is to an increasing extent being regarded as an integral part of urban planning with strong emphasis on the economic and social aspects. Discussions on planning are being transferred from the sphere of subsidiary sectoral goals to the sphere of the quality of life. The built environment is becoming one component among several in the arsenal of resources at the disposal of citizens as individuals and as groups. Qualitative issues are being pushed into the foreground and decentralization of decision-making is once more attracting interest. Public participation is seen as a valuable re-source in itself and also as a means of guiding future developments dominated by qualitative issues. Issues connected with the work environment, which also contain a strong element of construction work, are assuming the same amount of importance as the housing issue.

But regardless of trends in general, interest in community engineering has in-creased in step with increased interest in environmental protection and shortage of resources. The shortage of resources is drastically exemplified by the situa-tion in the energy sphere. Traffic, transport networks, water and sewerage, energy supply and solid waste handling are important technical spheres. And inside buildings a shift of interest is taking place away from questions of sta-bility and safety towards questions of climate and environment, i.e. from the load-bearing structure and climatic shell towards installations and spatial defining elements as a means of improving the environment and managing our energy resources.

This is not a uniform development perspective. In some countries, the background conditions outlined earlier still prevail and the shortage situation predominates. In addition, there are islands of shortage in all countries which need to be eli-minated by new construction. But if we look at the ECE area as a whole, we note that it manifests a sufficient measure of the new situation to justify the claim that a start has been made on changing the course.

The Situation Outside the ECE Area

It is scarcely sufficient to view developments exclusively from the standpoint of the industrialized and rich nations. The situation in the developing coun-tries also concerns us and influences our discussion on building research. Does not in fact their situation resemble that of the ECE countries after the war ? And is then the problem of mass-producing housing by industrialized methods not still the problem which also predominates in the field of building research ? Does not interest remain focussed on the problem of mass-production of dwellings, if we examine the issue from the point of view of the developing countries ?

During Habitat, the conference on human settlements held in 1976, the emphasis was on the position of the developing countries. The importance of an integrated development with economy, employment, social conditions and physical environment, all satisfactory balanced, was underlined. The workplace and the home were judged to be equally important. Land issues, public services such as transport, pure water supply, handling of solid waste and environmental protection were forced into the foreground. Shortage of resources drew attention to the importance of regarding existing buildings as a significant asset. Public participation was considered valuable, not only as part of the democratic decision-making process, but also as a decisive ingredient in the material conception of new housing construction. The construction and management of individual buildings constitute the parts of the total building process which individual persons may take part in. The contributions of the community should therefore be shifted towards public utilities, and will have their focus in planning, land issues, and the creation of infrastructures including workplaces, transport facilities, water supply and so on.

Obviously, there are big differences in the problems of the rich and poor countries respectively. However, it is also strikingly apparent that increased emphasis on far-reaching and composite issues in which housing construction is one ingredient among several with multitude of mutual correlations is becoming a common feature of development perspectives for industrialized and developing countries alike. Widening the range to include developing countries will largely strengthen the impression that industrial mass-production of housing is only a solution which can be applied successfully under the conditions which have prevailed in the ECE countries.

ORGANIZATION, STAFFING
AND FINANCING:
(PART II)

ORGANIZATIONAL STRUCTURE AND MANPOWER
RESOURCES OF BUILDING RESEARCH

G. Kunszt (rapporteur), Hungary

INTRODUCTION

Scientific policies are and always have to be related to the organizational
structure and manpower resources of the given research field. No scientific
policy can ever be realized without researchers who carry out the programmes
decided upon and without an organizational framework with adequate facilities.
Decisions on the goals and priorities of research should be closely followed
by decisions to provide an adequate organizational framework, equipment and
manpower; without careful planning and timely realization of these conditions
even the most brilliant programme will remain illusory. Besides, this task is
of serious concern, not only when an organization to implement building policy
has to be created practically from nothing, but also when an organizational
system with a long past and diversified structure is in question. Nothing can
be more inhibiting to the realization of a radically new research programme,
revealing bright prospects for the future, than a rigid organizational structure and an indifferent research staff, originally established according to the
requirements of other eras. Owing to their inherent inertia an organizational
structure and a professional hierarchy once established would be inclined to
prolong their own existence endlessly and resist any radical change. In an
unfavourable case, the existing organizational structure may react so unfortunately to any innovation that it may impede the solution of current problems
and the conception of progressive scientific policies.

In view of this negative outlook the evaluation of the research base (organizational structure and manpower) and the planning of its further development is
a fundamental task.

Since 1973, the ECE Committee on Housing, Building and Planning has followed the
policies related to building research with particular interest. The International Council of Building Research (CIB) began to deal with the problems of
the management of building research in the middle of the 1960s. ECE and CIB
activities in this field have produced a number of studies and other documents
providing extensive information on the status, organization and other characteristics of building research in ECE countries.

ORGANIZATIONAL STRUCTURE OF BUILDING RESEARCH IN ECE COUNTRIES

Among others, the documents mentioned above show that building research is
firmly based in all ECE countries. In most of them there is at least one
building research institute established and sponsored by the government, which
is independent both of industrial firms and of universities. In many countries
the number of independent building research institutes (and information centres)
established and sponsored by the State is about ten. In the USSR this figure
is of the order of one hundred. In countries with market economies the number
and role of government-established and sponsored institutes is (relatively)

smaller than in countries with centrally planned economies. In decisively
market-oriented countries, however, the research and development laboratories
and departments of industrial firms play more important parts. The role and
the performance of university institutes and laboratories in the field of building research are important everywhere, irrespective of the economic system.
In several countries the academies of science and scientific institutes also
play major parts. Academies have closer contacts with university or government-
sponsored research, while the associations favour contacts with industrial research. The number of staff (including supporting staff and clerical employees)
amounts, even in the smallest and least developed countries, to a few hundred
and in many countries to a few thousand. In the largest countries it even considerably exceeds ten thousand. It is therefore self-explanatory why it is no
easy task to survey building research activities on the national economy level.

SYSTEMS ANALYSIS AND MODELLING OF NATIONAL SYSTEMS OF BUILDING RESEARCH

In the past decade it has become common to refer to intricate organizational
structures such as those of building research organizations as "systems" and to
apply the methods of "systems analysis" to identify their problems.

According to C.W. Churchman* when speaking of a system the following five basic
considerations should be kept in mind.

- the system objectives
- the system's environment
- the resources of the system
- the components of the system
- the management of the system

With regard to building research this system has three basic components: governmental, university and industrial research. Naturally, each of these is
(or can be) broken down into various institutions, which further subdivide into
organizational units, e.g. research institutes and laboratories subdivide into
research divisions, departments, groups, etc.

The basic resources of the system are the available manpower, the buildings and
equipment of research laboratories (measuring instruments, computers, libraries,
etc.) as well as the funds (grants, contracts, etc.) necessary for financing
research and maintaining research institutions.

The system's environment includes enterprises of the construction and manufacturing industry, organizations for architectural design, building regulations,
quality control and product information, university and high school education,
the various types of building owners, the government and its policy, etc.

The system objectives are stated by specifying and analysing research goals and
priorities, while to identify the management it is necessary to clarify by whom,
how and based on what information the decisions fundamentally affecting the
operation of the system are made.

---

*C.W. Churchman: The Systems Approach, Dell Publishing Co., New York, 1968.

A usual method of systems analysis is the modelling of the system, the purpose
of which may be to clarify the relations between the system and its environment
on the one hand, and between the components of the system on the other, to
study the information flow between the system and its environment as well as
within the system, to survey and weigh the decision criteria typical within
the system, etc. The usual mathematical or quasi-mathematical form of rela-
tional models is the undirected graph and that of information flow models is
the directed graph; decision models are formulated most often with the aid
of equations or systems of equations (or inequalities and systems of inequalities). The special mathematical discipline established to work out the optimization techniques of decision models is operational research.

Although according to general opinion the direct application of mathematical
methods in the field of research management is seldom successful, it is remarkable how few indications can be seen in the literature on systems analysis
and operational research of concern with the management problems of building
research. Literature on the problems of the management of building research
has therefore been characterized by a general lack of systems approach and a
scarcity of efforts to model the organizational structure, information flow
and decision-making processes of building research. This statement applies
particularly to comprehensive national systems of building research: the
investigations carried out and published so far have been conducted almost
exclusively on the institute level.

It should be noted that reluctance to apply systems approach and modelling is
not an inherent characteristic of building and the building industry: e.g.
two significant CIB symposia, in Oslo in 1968 and Rotterdam in 1970, were
devoted to the problem of information flow in the building industry. Relative
lack of coverage in the building field is rather a characteristic of research
and innovation only. This can presumably be attributed to the fact that efforts
to manage building research and innovation on nation-wide level are relatively
weak or even missing.

RELATIONS BETWEEN SUBSYSTEMS AND THE PROBLEM OF MATRIX ORGANIZATION

We have shown above that the national system of building research has generally
three main components, or subsystems, governmental, university and industrial
research. The relations between these subsystems are rather indefinite in
many countries and a national system of building research therefore exists
only in a limited sense; a national system is an idea rather than a reality.
At the same time, a thorough investigation may show that relations between the
elements of the subsystems are often not much more convincing. Rivalry frequently occurs between governmental building research institutes (if, owing to
specialization, there are several of them in a country), mainly in fields where
several institutes consider themselves competent. There may exist wide differences of professional opinion between university chairs and institutes; eventual personal conflicts between professors may often upset even intramural co-
operation. Industrial research is frequently undertaken by competitors mutually
concealing their research projects which, if successful, enable them to offer
a better product or to cut down production costs. Last but not least it must
be pointed out that in major research institutes difficulties may arise owing
to internal isolation tendencies. This means that the relations between subsystems and between the elements of the subsystems are rather problematic at
all levels within the national system of building research. In such circumstances it is a particularly difficult organizational task to maintain an adequate information flow in the national system and even more difficult to spe-

cify and realize particular goals concerning the system as a whole.

A characteristic problem of the organizational structure of building research institutes is that of the so-called matrix organization as dealt with e.g. by the Copenhagen meeting of the CIB Working Commission W54 in 1975. An organizational question inherent in this problem is whether it is expedient to develop the divisions, departments, groups, etc. of building research institutes as disciplines or as project-oriented units. The reality lying in the background of the problem is that the major tasks emerging from the practice of building research and development institutions are in general of complex, interdisciplinary character in that they demand the co-ordinated effort of a number of disciplines in order to achieve a solution. Interdisciplinarity is as characteristic of the innovative tasks of building research as of the problems of the technological assessment of building.

Obviously in the organizational principles of management of building research institutes both orientation towards the major tasks of building practice as well as orientation towards scientific disciplines should equally prevail. The supervision and control of researchers in terms of a discipline is a primary condition of securing professional competence. Interdisciplinary problem-orientation is, on the other hand, a token of successful combined efforts on the part of the institutes. In mathematical terms this two-fold organizational requirement can be expressed by arranging the researchers of the institute into the cells of a matrix, the columns, say, of which are the scientific disciplines underlying the professional competence of the institute, while its rows represent combined research and development tasks, serving the actual practice of building, as specified by the supervisory authorities and/or sponsors.

In spite of the plausibility of this twofold requirement the structure of many research institutes in most countries is organized by discipline and hardly reflects the actual, complex problems which industry or society expect research institutes to solve. This can be explained by the fact that the lifetime of scientific disciplines is generally much longer than that of complex research projects; projects are often, disciplines hardly ever, replaced by others, which is also reflected by the organizational schemes of the institutes.

Unfortunately, one-sided structuring by discipline can often be attributed to further reasons; either to the lack of really large-scale programmes requiring an interdisciplinary approach or to the incompetence of the institutes to deal with such programmes. It may be possible to break down complex programmes into partial ones by discipline; however, research institutes usually fail to integrate the partial solutions.

Matrix organization can naturally be applied not only on an institutional but also on a nation-wide basis. In that case the various research institutes, as a rule profiled by discipline, should be taken as the columns, and the overall nation-wide research-development programmes as the rows of the matrix. The rows and columns, respectively, contain information on the programmes to be realized and on the institutes participating in the programmes. If the cells of the matrix contain appropriate indices of research inputs (costs, man years, etc.) we obtain a quantified model of the national system of building research which may be a fundamental tool of nation-wide surveys and further planning.

THE SUBSYSTEMS OF INFORMATION AND MANAGEMENT IN THE NATIONAL SYSTEM OF BUILDING RESEARCH

A primary condition of national-level management of building research is the establishment of an adequate research information system. This system should be a suitable source of information for researchers, its basic task is, however, to orientate government-level management on projects completed or initiated by the national network of building research. Many people think that government-level management cannot descend to the level of projects requiring an input of between 0.5 and 10 man/years. It is assumed that government level management can only orientate itself on the level of large-scale national programmes, generally of the order of some hundred man/years. This opinion is highly questionable: orientation in too wide terms does not provide sufficient information on the structure of the individual programmes, and does not reveal relations and possibly significant overlaps between them. Undoubtedly, however, to survey some hundred or thousand projects and to analyse the structure determined by the totality of the projects can hardly be imagined by merely manual means, but requires the computerized aid of survey and analysis. For this purpose, the computerized retrieval systems developed and applied as a routine in library science can be used to advantage. Even a "Keyword in context" (KWIC) index, processing project titles only, may offer much information for management on interrelations between the work undertaken in the national system and on the co-ordinator's tasks. There exist, however, much more sophisticated computerized systems, facilitating many-sided in-depth analysis. Such are e.g. the LOGEL system worked out in Hungary, based on the investigations of logical graphs obtainable by the key-word indexing of research projects. These methods of investigation make it possible to couple the topical and organizational structure of building research on the national level, laying the foundations for the evaluation of the organizational structure.

It is the first and most important task of government level management to state the goals and priorities of research on a nation-wide basis. For this purpose the information system considered above can be used with its input data completed by information on research needs, requirements and ideas. This information is to be obtained partly from the environment of the national system of building research, partly from the components of this system in the form of suitably formulated questionnaires, research concepts and proposals. On the basis of the processing of this information the formulation of a long or short term national research plan can be initiated, during the course of which a number of other factors should be taken into account: the position and perspectives of the national economy, the rights and obligations deriving from international co-operation, etc. In the preparatory stage of the plan it is expedient for more refined deliberations to be undertaken by specialized professional committees, which can later be entrusted with the management and control of the realization of priority programmes. These committees and other bodies capable of organizing government level planning and supervisory activities constitute the top stratum of the structure of the building research system, i.e. government level management. This managerial organizational stratum must possess adequate power, funds and other means (e.g. the use of news media, the right to reshape university education programmes, etc.) to be able to promote the implementation of the goals of nation-wide scientific policy. In addition to direct governmental instructions, economic motivation systems and influence exerted on the outlook of researchers may also be of decisive importance. Naturally, the organization and methods of management required depend on the perspectives of building research in the country concerned: programmes aimed at revolutionary quantitative and qualitative changes require strong management machinery, while a slight polishing up to traditional methods may be expected from the self-regulating mechanism of the research market.

BASIC TRAINING OF RESEARCHERS

The ECE document (HBP/WP.2/R.56) referred to in paragraph 3 of the present paper pointed out the problems of training building researchers. The first difficulty lies in university education.

Building research – as a particular field of science – falls primarily into the category of applied research. University education – on the level of all sciences – has already been subject to numerous appraisals from the point of view of researcher training.

The failure of university education to do anything for the research-methodological training of students entering applied research has provoked the sharpest criticism.* It is mainly due to the fact that the overwhelming majority of university professors are basic-research-oriented and generally have few contacts with industrial (applied) research. This circumstance naturally also affects building research, but owing to other reasons the situation in this field is still more unfavourable.

We have pointed out above the interdisciplinary character of the innovation and assessment tasks of building research, which should involve not only architects, structural engineers, and civil engineers who have received comprehensive orientation during their university education on the problems of building and building research, but chemists, physicists, mechanical engineers, electronic engineers, sociologists and psychologists who received hardly any information on building industrial production during their university education. Among them, the chemists and physicists normally have a certain basic knowledge of the methodology of fundamental research. However, building research is actually applied research, and they do not know the industry either in which the results of their work could be expected to be utilized. Architects and structural and civil engineers know more of the building industry but have rather underdeveloped notions of science, in contrast to the average graduate, of any kind of scientific discipline.

The consequence is that if an interdisciplinary building research team were to be composed of architects, engineers and scientists who have just graduated, that team would be almost incapable of dealing with any research task in the field of building.

Investigations are also required on the international level as to what steps should be taken to improve the development of building research at the level of university education and in the background professions. The most radical change is called for in the training of architects because in the majority of interdisciplinary building research teams the leading role should be allocated to an architect, which requires architects to be trained especially for interdisciplinary research work.

The most important subjects of this post-graduate training of architects could be the following:

---

*See e.g.: P. Papon: "The training of industrial scientists in France", Minerva, London 1973, Vol. 11, No. 2.

- general system theory and introduction into operational research

- theory of building systems

- research into the future of urban planning and building

- problems and methods of interdisciplinary research.

POSTGRADUATE TRAINING

Owing to the deficiencies of basic university education some other forms of training for researchers and scientists are especially vital in building research. The most essential of these are:

- introduction of new researchers into research technologies at the work place

- postgraduate training of researchers at the universities

- training of scientists under the scientific degrees system.

Regarding the training to be offered to new recruited researchers the informal impacts they receive from their environment at their new workplace are of decisive importance. Many institutes organize formal introductory courses, little information is, however, available on the subject-matter of these courses and the experience gained with them. In this field, an international exchange of experience could also be useful, which CIB Working Commission W54 might be suitably invited to organize.

Postgraduate university training (or university level training) is a type of specialist training also applied in the field of building. In Hungary, two-year courses have been organized on several occasions for the training of building physicists, for engineers specializing in prefabrication, in the testing of materials and structures and in urban planning.

The engineers of developing countries are offered postgraduate training in several European countries (Netherlands, France and elsewhere). Similar courses have been organized under the auspices of the various United Nations organizations.

Profound professional knowledge enables those who have completed these courses to carry out research work, there is, however, little sign of whether the organizers of these courses have devoted sufficient attention to training candidates in research technology. In this respect it would be justified to initiate action on behalf of the ECE or UNESCO.

The awarding of scientific degrees, a work organized and regulated in most countries on government level, can be regarded as an important form of researcher training. Interesting activities are in progress in this field, also in building research, all over Europe. Governments may do a great deal to improve the efficiency of this system by granting moral and financial support for working out projects essential from the point of view of national building science policy. In certain regions there is an international system of awarding degrees, e.g. in the eastern European socialist countries. This development is highly advantageous as it promotes personal contacts between the scientists of the various countries; it would thus be expedient to recommend and support it on the ECE level. In several countries, critics of the system of awarding scientific degrees have primarily disapproved of the fact that it was motivating individual efforts rather than promoting the improvement of interdisciplinary team work. On several occasions objections were raised, on the one hand, to the failure of candidates working for a degree to maintain sufficiently close contact with the basic research problems of their countries and on the other, to the artificial problems often dealt with in such circumstances.

In the field of building, research management education is also a problem to be solved. The Centre for Management Education of the Hungarian Ministry of Building and Urban Development has recently worked out a proposal for the organization of this training in Hungary.

CREATIVITY AND PRODUCTIVITY: RECRUITMENT AND ADJUSTMENT

In addition to recruiting researchers of adequate qualifications it is an equally important task of manpower development to recruit researchers of adequate creativity. According to a test carried out earlier at the Building Research Station in the United Kingdom* the success of research at the Station was rather a function of the general ability of the researcher responsible for the project than of his research skills and knowledge of the subject. Probably this statement does not apply to all types of research, however, it points out that, in planning and managing research, the persons actually responsible for the research and their abilities cannot be disregarded. It should even be emphasized that in many respects everything depends on this.

In research psychology different types of tests have been worked out**which attempt to assess creativity on the basis of suitable measurements of the fluency, flexibility and originality of the intellect.

Though it is not very probable that such formal tests will be applied for recruiting building researchers in the near future, their informal application may be justified because many research managers and personnel department heads overestimate the qualifications and previous jobs of candidates.

At the same time, the statements of research sociology cannot be disregarded either, according to which the productivity of researchers does not depend on their creativity only but also on a number of environmental and moral factors. The creativity climate of the workplace is usually an intricate reality, which a good manager should attempt to analyse, because a bad environment may ruin or at least severely deform even the best of talents. According to general opinion productivity is some basic harmony between the creative man and his environment on the one hand, and the cultural and social system constituting the wider environment on the other. Servile conformity has, however, a paralysing effect.

The adjustment of new researchers to the organization also gives rise to a number of problems.*** It is quite normal that the uncertainty of the first

---

*J.B. Dick: "Effectiveness of some recent research at the Building Research Station, United Kingdom", Build International, November 1968.
**See e.g. J.P. Guilford: "Three faces of intellect", The American Psychologist, 1959, No. 8.
***C.C. Bucher: "How to help the new researcher adjust to the organization", Research Management, New York, 1974, No. 4.

weeks is followed by an increased feeling of failure, mainly due to the lack of orientation in bureaucratic channels and to failure in recognizing and accepting the limitations imposed by the organization. In several socialist countries the so-called "Youth Act" makes it an obligation of managements to help young people adjust and solve their personal research problems. This naturally requires managerial knowledge of human relations and a recognition and appreciation of their significance, which is an important subject of and, at the same time, the reason for research management education.

MOTIVATION

In addition to recruiting researchers of adequate qualifications and creativity, a fundamental requirement is the adequate motivation of the researchers' activities. To survey the various possible levels of motivation Maslow's motivation theory based on the hierarchy of needs can be used to advantage.*

In this concept, according to the interpretation of G.C. Bucher and R.C. Gray,** higher needs are activated as lower ones are satisfied. At the lowest level of the hierarchy stand physiological needs (food, shelter, etc.) which, proceeding upwards, are followed by safety needs and at the next higher level by belongingness and love needs. At the fourth level of Maslow's hierarchy stand needs in connexion with the individual's self-esteem and reputation, such as self-confidence, independence, competence, knowledge, etc., on the one part, and status, recognition, appreciation, respect from fellow employees etc. on the other.

At the topmost level of the hierarchy stand self-fulfilment needs, "the needs for achieving one's potentials, for continued self-development and for being creative in the broadest sense".** As a matter of fact "self-actualization needs may be dormant in most humans because of their struggles to satisfy lower-order needs".** The levels of needs are independent and overlapping, with the higher need levels emerging before the lower need levels have been completely satisfied.

It is now obvious that the correct strategy of motivation starts from realistically taking into account the hierarchy structure of needs even if Maslow's concept of the adjustment pattern of the individual - and social-psychological motives could not be regarded as fully satisfactory. In all actual cases of motivation it should be examined on which level of the hierarchy of needs the persons or strata to be motivated are the most strongly activated and the steps of motivation should be planned on that level. In principle, the motivation of the most talented and valuable persons is the most effective on the uppermost level of the hierarchy, it would, however, be useless and even false to appeal to this level in connexion with persons suffering from severe unsolved problems at the lower levels of needs. On the other hand, offering salary increase and promotion may arouse dislike and even resistance from persons for whom being prevented from creative self-fulfilment is the most severe problem and for whom only increased independence and freedom in research work, and the acceptance and support of their deepest and most intimate research impulses would be of real value.

---

*A.H. Maslow: Motivation and personality, Harper and Row, New York, 1954.
**G.C. Bucher; R.C. Gray: "The principles of motivation and how to apply them", Research Management, New York, 1971, No. 5.

In any case management should take advantage of these refined means of motivation just as consciously as of the more current means of salary increase and
promotion. An effective version of financial reward is offered by motivation
systems granting researchers the personal right to apply for patents and to
share a considerable portion of the profit deriving from the patent. It is an
effective motivation in the scientific degrees system to allocate to the recipient a certain amount of monthly allowance. It is also an effective financial
and moral incentive to reward outstanding scientific work by valuable prizes
offered by the State or the professional associations.

PERFORMANCE MEASUREMENT AND CAREER DEVELOPMENT

Financial and moral reward equally raise the methodological problem of assessment and evaluation of the researcher's performance. Quantitative characteristics are also used (number of publications, citations), however, everybody
agrees that these do not in themselves provide a reliable basis for assessment.
Among the qualitative characteristics, the originality as well as the theoretical and practical significance of research findings are usually emphasized.
An effective method of appraisal is a scientific discussion involving the best
competent researchers and practical experts. In an institutional form, inviting
paid opponents, this is the common practice of many of the institutes in most
east European countries. The opponent's task consists in pointing out the deficiencies of the report to be discussed at the meeting by working out a written
professional opinion and in attempting to assess the value of the report. The
opponents' comments contribute a great deal to the liveliness of the debates
although personal conflicts or prejudice may distort even these comments.

There are countries (e.g. Hungary) where the so-called "qualification" of
researchers is a government-regulated system. This is a written evaluation
covering some longer (e.g. 3-5 year) period of a researcher's scientific activities and attitude towards his colleagues, specifying the scientific and human
requirements regarding his further development. This written qualification is
prepared by the researcher's supervisor, and discussed with the researcher in
the presence of the director and the head of the personnel department. The
result of the discussion is put on record.

Organized aid and planning for researchers' careers are generally thought to
be essential in the literature. According to Bucher and Gray "it is critical
to assist young scientists in establishing challenging goals which help them
mature. The supervisor might assign an older more experienced scientist as
a mentor for the young scientist. After technical maturity has been demonstrated, the supervisor should give the scientist a chance to work alone on a
problem, possibly by shifting him to a new project and possibly to a new supervisor and new colleagues. It is also desirable to encourage the scientist who
has reached the midcareer point to reorient himself, possibly by a sabbatical
leave to attend a university. This will help the individual establish new goals
and objectives for himself, with resulting benefits to the organization".*

MANPOWER INFORMATION

Scientific research is of outstanding importance from the point of view of the
future of mankind and it is therefore necessary that governments pay special

---

*G.C. Bucher; R.C. Gray: "The principles of motivation and how to apply them",
Research Management, New York, 1971, No. 5.

attention to scientific researchers. Government activities in this field are
aided by a highly important UNESCO document, containing recommendations on the
status of scientific researchers.*

These recommendations urge governments to specify in writing the requirements
applicable to, and the rights vested in, researchers and to have every researcher read this document before entering work.

The requirements to be applied to scientific researchers are determined by an
order of the Committee for Science Policy of the Government of the Hungarian
People's Republic, authorizing ministers to formulate special requirements
applicable to particular fields of research.

A field of research deserving special attention is that of building research,
on which depends to a great extent whether the towns, dwellings, communal, industrial and other buildings of the future will form a technically adequate
environment worthy of man. The researchers in the building field, tne manpower
from whom the solution of the research problems of building can be expected,
deserve particular attention.

The national system of information and management mentioned above should take
into account the available manpower with a breakdown referring to researchers.
In addition to project files it is also necessary to maintain personal files,
providing orientation on the special knowledge and fields of interest of researchers.

When launching especially large-scale and up-to-date national building research
programmes it may be necessary not to rely primarily on a given organizational
structure but on the manpower actually available, taking directly from this
stock a group of persons capable of solving the new problem. The updating of
the existing organizational structure should be carried out on the basis of the
proposals of this problem-oriented group. On the other hand, if an institute
has to change over to new tasks, it is expedient to reorganize its staff mainly
on the basis of this central information system. These can be regarded as the
most striking cases of the interaction between the organizational structure and
the manpower resources of building research.

POINTS FOR DISCUSSION

Reasons and methods for the national harmonization of governmental, university
and industrial building research. Justification of an organizational method
applied by large-scale national research projects in the field of building.

The benefit and findings of systems analysis in establishing and developing a
national system of building research. The role of computers in research information and government level management.

The development of university education and postgraduate training to improve the
manpower available for building research. The most important general and special
subjects in the training of building researchers and research management.

Best methods for the appraisal and motivation of the performance of researchers.
Adequate criteria for the selection of research directors, managers and super-
visors.

---

*Recommendation on the status of scientific researchers, UNESCO, Paris, 1974.

Inconsistencies in national building research policy and programme as well as in the organizational and staff structure and how to resolve them. The obsolescence of scientific disciplines, research subjects, researchers and managers, the development of new disciplines and subjects and the acceleration of their development.

DISSEMINATION OF INFORMATION AND UTILIZATION OF RESEARCH RESULTS (PART I)

V. G. Lastotchkin (rapporteur), Byelorussian SSR

INFORMATION SYSTEM FOR RESEARCH RESULTS

In the Byelorussian SSR building is one of the most dynamically developing industrial branches. In this connexion, a timely dissemination of information on research results, aiming at their effective and the most expedient utilization, is getting a particular importance.

In the Byelorussian SSR this field of activities is in care of scientific-technical information institutions. Information on the results of research work fulfilled on direct contracts with building bodies is transferred directly to these bodies by executor-institutes.

Brief information on the results of all research work is accumulated at the Byelorussian Institute for Scientific Information and Technico-Economic Research (BelNIINTI) of the State Planning Committee subordinate to the Byelorussian SSR Council of Ministers. This ensures prompt computer retrieval of the necessary documentation referring to any research results. The BelNIINTI transfers annotated lists, giving information on the results of research, experimental and design work in the construction field, to the Institute for Building and Architecture subordinate to the BSSR GOSSTROY; then this information is communicated to all bodies concerned for practical utilization. This system of scientific and technical information avoids duplication when planning research and design work and allows for more complete information on the results of activities in the construction field.

The scientific-technical information value is determined by the two main factors: its "freshness" and readiness for an immediate practical utilization.

It is quite clear that the shorter the time gap between the research results achievement and the information reception the more valuable the information will be. The Byelorussian SSR experts think that in building the optimum term for information to give effect, when it is not undergoing moral aging, does not exceed two years. If the time gap between the completion of research work and the realization of its results is longer the information loses its actuality and the results realized get an ordinary character. This, of course, is not related to the information on the basic theoretical research results which in some cases can influence the development of this or that scientific trend for many years.

All building research can conditionally be divided into two categories:

- category A - basic research developing the existing theoretical ideas;
- category B - applied research, resulting in practical suggestions (new building structures, technological methods, etc.)

Information on research results of the category A is usually used by the institutes themselves for improving the theoretical level of research and hence its effectiveness. Information on research results of the category B is used by the industrial organizations. That's why it can be useful only in cases when research results are ready for their immediate practical utilization. The information in question is to be transmitted in the form of specifications on new structures, technology, design methods, computer programmes, etc.

Even with the high quality of information provided one should have an efficient direct and back communication between the information suppliers and users. Existence of such communication (stage of industrial realization of research is included) gives the opportunity to insert the necessary amendments in time and reduces the risk of possible moral and material losses.

Evaluation of information use efficiency is facilitated by the existence of direct and back communication between the information suppliers and users. In the Byelorussian SSR organizations and enterprises, having used scientific and technical information, are obliged, after a two year term (possible time of research results implementation and achievement of sensible effects) to inform both the information suppliers and the governmental institutions, controlling the given branch, about the results achieved. Existence of such a system gives the possibility of a thorough control of the information use efficiency and thus the efficiency of research.

As a rule, economic efficiency of research is estimated at 3 stages: potential economic effect is determined tentatively at the planning stage, more exact potential economic effect is estimated on the accomplishment of research and at last, after a certain period of research results implementation, one can determine actual economic effect achieved. Efficiency criteria are the following: cutting of production costs and labour-consuming nature of building, reduction of specific capital investment expenses and material resources.

In the Byelorussian SSR careful attention in the evaluation of research results is given to the social effect together with indicators of economic and technical progress.

INFORMATION METHODS

The following 3 types of information on the results of completed research deserve consideration:

> concise annotated lists and statistic data, submitted to statistic and planning governmental bodies;

> detailed reports, submitted to governmental institutions controlling the given branch;

> prospectus, giving information on the main points of research, expected economic effect and the address of the institute having accomplished the research work for the interested industrial organizations.

Alongside the official sources of information, special technical journals serve the same purpose. Data on the experience of scientific research results introduction into construction are usually published there.

In the Byelorussian SSR the journal "STROITELSTVO I ARKHITEKTURA BELORUSSII" is published where under the special heading one can find articles on the most successful results of scientific research work in building.

One of the active forms of information is an organization of thematic exhibitions with the demonstration of practical results of research in the form of structures, models of technological lines, new structural materials, etc.

It would be useful for the further development in this field to organize international exhibitions of achievements in building industry regularly at 5-year intervals. We consider it useful to organize such an exhibition in the nearest future.

PROBLEMS OF RESEARCH RESULTS UTILIZATION

Up to now there has been formed the traditional scheme of research development: idea - theoretical grounding of the idea - experimental test of the idea - engineering development - practical test - putting into production. The Byelorussian SSR experts consider that research should not be finished by the practical test of the results achieved. One can be sure of the complete realization of the idea only in case when scientists participate in its putting into production up to the achievement of stable results.

In view of this, the system of the so-called scientific - industrial complexes is very expedient. Under such system the development of the theme is realized jointly by researchers on a par with engineering staff of an industrial organization concerned with the final results.

This very form of technical and scientific co-operation is widely spreading in the Byelorussian SSR. So, e.g., for the development of the very efficient for the Republic theme on the creation of centrifuged columns, the efforts of the Byelorussian Polytechnical Institute scientists were united with those of the industrial trust directly concerned with the results of the work. It made it possible to begin mass production of new structures in 2 years, that ensured in its turn a 40 per cent economy of concrete and 20 per cent of steel in comparison with traditional methods.

Concentration of creative efforts and material means of the solution of important scientific-practical problems in building is one of the trends in research policy in the BSSR. To achieve this aim, several institutes which work under the co-ordinative guidance of the head institute are involved in the solution of an important scientific problem. This complex approach to the solution of the problem makes it possible to shorten considerably the time of research.

The Government of the Republic has adopted the resolution on programme-task planning and financing of research work. It will give the opportunity to solve the important problems of technical progress in different branches of people's economy in complex, and to more closely link research with practical needs.

Taking into consideration the fact that perfection of the research policy is a long-term process, the problem should be somehow reflected in the materials of seminars conducted under the guidance of the ECE Working Party on the Building Industry. In this connexion, it is necessary that the published materials of every seminar had a section devoted to the most important research results achieved in the given branch of the building industry. Here the results which are of practical interest for the majority of the ECE member countries are meant (decrease of harmful influence of building on the environment, possibilities for energy resources conservation, creation of new structural materials, etc.).

Aiming at the co-ordination of the efforts on perfection of the research policy in building, the governments of the ECE member countries and international bodies should be recommended to more effectively organize the regular informa- tion exchange on the given problem.

DISSEMINATION OF INFORMATION AND UTILIZATION OF RESEARCH RESULTS

D.A. Senior (rapporteur)

Assistant Director of Research Policy, Departments of the Environment and Transport, United Kingdom

INTRODUCTION

This paper examines some of the factors involved in formulating policies aimed at promoting the utilization of the results of research and development in the building field. No attempt is made to give complete coverage since it seems more useful to explore a number of basic issues and problems which concern all the countries taking part in this seminar and which are being resolved in different ways or with different emphases.

A consideration of the unity of research and application is followed by some observations on the organization of research and the needs of the users of the results. This leads to an examination of the general problems of dissemination, principles and current practice. Finally shortcomings and possible remedies are discussed and the conclusion is reached that there is a need for a better understanding of the ways in which decision-makers become aware of and react to technological information. The argument is illustrated by examples of United Kingdom practice which are given in the form of annexes.

The Research and Application Process

The main concern of this paper is the dissemination process which is regarded as part of a cycle in which goals for **research** are established, appropriate research is carried out, and the results are applied, leading in time to new needs and new goals. To be rather more precise, dissemination is part of a great number of research/application cycles which are and indeed should be interrelated.

Such a view of applied research is generally accepted nowadays as a useful model, but it is worth remembering that it is the result of historical development. In the early stages, a much simpler view was taken of the research/application system, and indeed one of the first problems was to convince potential users that technical data could benefit such a traditional industry as that of building. Since then, stimulation of the demand for research, its expansion, its increasing sophistication, and its broadening into new fields such as planning and construction economics have led to a much greater complexity in the relations between researchers and their clients. More and more often a single piece of research serves more than one identified goal; thinking is more in terms of systems; and research managers are increasingly involved, though still on a modest scale, in government policy making.

Thus, it is no longer sufficient, if it ever was, merely to publish the results of research on materials and processes of construction. Nor is it now enough to set up machinery to "sell" the results. It is doubtful even if the marketing approach in which effort is devoted to a systematic study of the needs of the market is sufficient. It is becoming increasingly evident that

41

every piece of research must be viewed individually and the appropriate forms
of co-operation between supplier and user of research results devised accordingly. Close co-operation between research and user interests is essential
throughout the whole cycle of goal-setting, research, dissemination, application and feed-back to future goal-setting. The demand on the creativity of
the research worker is just as great, but he must now be involved as never
before in dissemination of the results.

The importance accorded to dissemination activities can be judged from the
effort currently devoted to it. In the United Kingdom Building Research
Establishment, for example, dissemination now absorbs nearly half as much
effort as does the research itself. This should be regarded as no cause for
satisfaction or regret: the only reasonable aim is to optimize the return
for effort expended in the whole process, which will now be examined in more
detail with research as a convenient starting point.

The Research Organization
Whilst at one time research relevant to building was carried out at a
relatively small number of centres, the activity is now generally much more
widespread. This is certainly true of the United Kingdom (1)* though it may
not be true of all the countries participating in the seminar.

A wide spread of research activity has advantages and disadvantages. It
permits research to be carried out near to the point of application, so mini-
mizing communication problems, for goal-setting as well as dissemination of
results. For example, research aimed at improving a company's competitive
position has the best chance of success, if it is carried out within the
company, or at least in an "industrial environment", whilst work related to
the generality of regulation and control is best carried out in national
organizations. On the other hand, the wide distribution of research activity
has undoubtedly introduced problems of communication between researchers or
more particularly research policy makers, as witness the frequency with which
the same topic is discussed in various committees, sometimes with the same
individuals participating. Fragmentation of research has in practice mili-
tated against the interdisciplinary or system approach which is increasingly
needed in dissemination as well as in the carrying out of research itself,
though there is no reason why this must be so in principle.

There are no easy solutions because centralization of research introduces
problems through the lengthening of the lines of communication whilst
excessive "rationalization" and "elimination of duplication" can adversely
affect the liveliness of research. One can only aim at the best balance,
setting up and giving adequate support to liaison arrangements between members
of the various research organizations but reviewing these frequently as needs
change.

The Users
The ultimate beneficiary of building research and development is the general
public which for the most part receives its benefits so to speak at second
hand through the intermediary of decision-makers within regulating authorities,
the construction industry etc. Some special direct needs of the public have

---

*The numbers in brackets refer to headings in the annex.

to be catered for however. Concern has been expressed about what has been
called "technological decision-making behind closed doors" in government and
industry. Increasing public interest, and increasing activity of groups representing or claiming to represent the public interest in developments affecting
the environment seem bound to call for an increasing flow of information to
the public and to such groups. The information needs to be 100 per cent
reliable and as far as possible in a form that can be handled by the layman.
It seems inevitable that there will be increasing involvement of building
research organizations in the handling and dissemination of such information.

It is however the intermediaries, the decision-makers in government and
industry, who are the direct users of research, and the channels for dissemination of research results must be conditioned by the motives, terms of
reference and limitations of the users' organizations. The range of interests
is wide but a simple functional description will suffice to identify them for
present purposes. If these are listed in the same order as the building
sequence, first are the architects and other designers. Next must be
considered the organizations responsible for construction itself, ranging
from large construction companies to small building firms. The design and
construction functions may be separate, as frequently occurs in the United
Kingdom, or combined in the same firms. A considerable role in the building
process is played by the specialist sub-contractors responsible for such
matters as building services (heating, lighting, air-conditioning, plumbing
and drainage), decoration, roofing and flooring. Contractors and sub-contractors draw on the output of building materials producers, building component
manufacturers and plant manufacturers. All operate within a framework of
housing and planning policy and regulations evolved generally by central
government and applied by local government agencies. Serving the control
process are the organizations which are involved in the making of standards
and in certifying or assessing building products or processes (represented
in the United Kingdom by the British Standards Institution and the Agrément
Board for example) and the test houses.

The needs for research input vary widely (2) but some of the common factors
influencing dissemination can be identified. Taking the components of the
industry in the order in which they have been listed, the design function
represents a prime target for dissemination activity. The effectiveness of
the whole industry is highly dependent on the extent to which architects and
structural and other designers appreciate the principles of building practice
and understand their physical base. There is a great need for the translation of research results into simple design guides and for clear guidance on
the nature of commercial products and their suitability to various purposes.

As regards the industry, the differing responsibilities and motives of its
various parts, the interests of organized labour and the frequent dichotomy
between owner and user and between designer and builder, all influence application. They determine among other things attitudes to the relation between
initial costs and maintenance. There is also a sponsorship function exercised
by government in relation to the industry. It has two main elements: first
the identification of the interests of the industry and consideration of these
in the formulation of government policies, and second encouragement of the
efficiency of the industry, including its technical competence. In this
connexion, a problem exists with construction and manufacturing firms which
are too small to have high in-house technical competence. These firms benefit
from research through the medium of advice from material and components
suppliers and various advisory services, but the benefit of this advice is

limited when it depends on requests for help which such firms may not be in
a position to formulate. For this reason, technical advisory services have
been set up from time to time with a remit actively to promote technical
change and to act as liaison with other elements in the research and production system. Though this has had considerable success in the United Kingdom
with other industries, notably agriculture, its success with the United
Kingdom construction industry has been limited.

The industry derives benefit not only from research carried out on its behalf
but through the introduction of technology developed in other industries such
as plastics and chemicals. The manufacturers of components and materials
constitute a useful channel for the introduction of such technology.

Legislation has an important effect. For example, when the responsibilities
of the builder extend over a long period after construction, insurance
becomes more important and insurers have **greater need** for technical advice.
(This has led for example to the French Avis Technique).

Finally, the role of professional organizations and societies and that of
industrial federations should not be forgotten. These not only assist in the
dissemination of information but induce a certain spirit of emulation which
encourages the application of research.

Dissemination
The need for mutual understanding between research workers and those responsible for decisions leading to application has already been stressed (para. 5).
This need, among others, has led the United Kingdom to accept the so-called
customer/contractor principle as a basis for the organization of government
research and development. The matter·is primarily the concern of another
subject of this seminar but it is noteworthy in the context of dissemination
that representatives of contractors and customers (that is research workers
and users of research results respectively) in coming together to discuss the
formulation of research programmes have both benefited from greater understanding of each other's situation with consequent improvement in dissemination
of results. One of the reasons for this improvement is that the dialogue
assists the researcher to appreciate the non-technical problems which the user
faces.

It has to be remembered that recent research results usually represent only
a small proportion of the whole information employed by the user in his
decision making. Much of his data has often been available for a considerable
time and only some of it is technically based. This may account for what
seems sometimes to the researcher to be the user's negative attitude. Contact
can correct this impression and help the researcher to give more realistic
advice and to inspire confidence. The user must have the confidence whether
he be builder or administrator for in either case he may be required directly
or indirectly to commit considerable sums of money on the basis of the information and assessments he receives.

Personal contact is thus important but it is possible only on a small scale.
There are for example in the United Kingdom in round numbers 41,000 registered
architects, 12,000 members of the Institution of Structural Engineers, 1,500
building firms employing over 100 people and 80,000 employing less than 100.
Personal contact can therefore be made with only a limited number of users.
For the majority, indirect methods are needed and the success or failure of
these rests largely on the reputation for reliability and realism of the

source of information. Reputations are established over years and the most
sophisticated methods of dissemination are no substitute.

Principles of Technology Transfer

The complexity of the task is reflected in the range of activities involved in
dissemination. These have now widened to the point at which "technology
transfer" is perhaps a better term. Technology transfer is not so well
understood as it might be and there is a feeling that research application is
less effective in consequence. The understanding we have however had led to
a number of general principles and it seems worthwhile to enumerate these
briefly since it is through their testing and application that improvements
are to be sought. Some of these principles are summarized in the following
propositions:

Technology consists of both hardware and software. By hardware is meant
materials, components, plant, instruments etc., whilst software refers to
principles, practice and methods.

The use of technology depends on the environment in which it will operate (for
example the skills of those who carry out maintenance and repair or the public
acceptability of proposed policies).

Boundaries exist between one environment or institution and another. To be
applied, new technology arising from research must move across such boundaries,
which exist between the research laboratory and the user organization as well
as within the user and research organizations themselves.

Although the boundaries apparently hinder transfer processes, they are a
necessary feature of a modern industrial system since they provide protection
for the development of specific skills and knowledge.

Technology transfer can be regarded as having three components: transfer of
information, establishment of understanding and encouragement of attitudes.
Personal intervention is not very important for the first of these, but it is
more important for the second and seems most important for the third. The
speed with which personal contact can change attitudes, and so open the door
to improved efficiency of application is perhaps not always recognized.

The catalytic potential of research suggests that one should think less in
terms of dissemination which means the sowing of seeds, and more in terms of
leavening, that is the introduction of ferment. Such an approach implies
selectivity - viz. the favouring of users who will apply the results the most
effectively or have the most influence on others.

Technology transfer involves more than the simple shift of knowledge etc.,
from one environment to another. Accompanying innovation to adapt it to the
special needs of the user is also necessary. It follows that there must be
some disturbance of the system into which the technology is to enter. Use of
new technology always involves change, which can be unwelcome.

The adaptation of both the technology and the receiving system calls for the
existence in the receiving system of an adequate technological infrastructure,
that is an adequate stock of knowledge, technique, craft experience and know-
how much of which can never be made explicit.

Above all, technology transfer depends on the presence of adequate motivation

C

in the receiving organization.

If these propositions are accepted, it is salutary to examine our arrangements
in the light of them. For example, have we achieved an adequate balance
between the processing and general dissemination of information on the one
hand and the more active and selective modes such as personal contact on the
other ? How explicitly do we work out our strategy of influencing people in
key positions ? How much thought do we give to the problems of adaptation
within the receiving organization ?

It can be argued that major improvements are not likely to follow from
improvement in the machinery of dissemination but only from some restructuring
of the whole system of which dissemination is a small part.

Current Arrangements
Restructuring will only be brought about in the long run however. In the
meantime, optimization of technology transfer must be within existing constraints, and current arrangements can be generalized as follows: mandatory
instructions, specifications and standards; the educational system; publications, exhibitions, conferences and lectures; information and advisory
services; specific application services; "development groups" and the mobility of technologists. The remainder of this section is devoted to filling
in the detail under these headings, but one proposition is more important than
any of this detail. It is that none of the arrangements can operate effectively if the research worker fails to recognize his deep involvement in the
process of dissemination. It is primarily his responsibility to ensure that
potential users of research are approached - directly when this is possible.

First, codes of practice, instructions, specifications and standards. (3)
These can offer an excellent vehicle. When they are mandatory or virtually
mandatory (as when compliance with a code of practice is accepted as satisfying a legal requirement), application of research embodied in them is
assured; and specifications can be made more strict as knowledge and understanding advance. The research results secure wide application, but at the
expense of waiting for the next revision of the document concerned which can
introduce a delay of several years between research and application.

Second, the educational system. In the long run, this represents one of the
principal channels by which research results are incorporated in professional
practice. Establishments of higher education need continuously to revise
their curricula to take in new knowledge. Training courses and seminars
within research establishments are particularly valuable in this connexion.
The influencing of attitudes is perhaps as important as is the transfer of
information.

Third, publications, exhibitions, conferences and lectures. The variations
in each case are well known but several points seem worthy of note:

   (i)   The multiplicity of types of publication indicates the scale of
         the problems inherent in dissemination. Attempts are constantly
         being made to limit the range, if only to economize on storage
         and handling costs, but without great success it seems.
   (ii) It is important for results to be brought together in "state of
         the art" reviews or digests (expressed in terms relevant to the
         user's not the research worker's problems and often short, as

leaflets). United Kingdom experience suggests that specialist
research staff have a big role to play in producing material of
this sort, assisted by specialist editorial staff. There is a
problem in that the same work often needs to be written up in a
number of different ways for different audiences, and acceptance
is often achieved only after much repetition. Research workers
are reluctant to devote a great deal of time to this sort of work,
yet it is not easily done by others.

(iii) Participation by research establishments in exhibitions organized
for trade or other purposes provides a means of making chance
contact with individuals accessible by other means only with
difficulty and whose interest is general but significant. Site
demonstrations and open days (in which laboratories put on special
demonstrations and show illustrative material to selected visitors)
seem, however, generally more productive, though objective assessment is difficult.

(iv) Conferences and lectures are important not least because they
provide an opportunity for people with an inside knowledge of the
possibilities and limitations of research to meet those concerned
with using its results.

(v) Timing is sometimes very important. If research results are
produced too late, the work might as well not have been done; if
it is completed too soon the investment is earning no interest.
But the situation is usually less clear cut than this analysis
would imply. It is equally important for results to have special
publicity at a time when some outside event makes them clearly
relevant and publicity arrangements should be flexible enough for
advantage to be taken of such opportunities to influence attitudes
of both professionals and public.

Fourth, information and advisory services. These provide an essential means
of application of research results which are not highly specialized but which
have to be applied in the context of other information. It is important to
recognize three levels. At one level, information can be dispensed by non-
specialists usually by means of leaflets. This is best done in a practically
orientated ambiance closely associated with trade information as in building
centres. The second level is that of advice on more difficult problems given
not by specialists but by those closely associated with them; United Kingdom
experience suggests that if this activity is to be credible it has to be
centred on or very closely associated with the research organization. At a
third level is the advice which only the specialist can give. This includes
not only advice to practitioners in the forefront of technological advance but
also advice to high level government commissions of enquiry.

Fifth, specific application services. The need has already been mentioned for
every piece of research to be viewed individually and the appropriate forms of
co-operation between supplier and user of results devised accordingly. The
recognition of this need for positive action in research application is
perhaps a major change in kind which has occurred in recent years as opposed
to changes in degree, because the other arrangements which have been described,
though now having greater effort devoted to them, are all of relatively long
standing.

Because of the importance of this development, an Application Section (4) was
set up by the Building Research Establishment of the United Kingdom some years
ago to adapt and develop marketing techniques and to apply these where they

would be most effective either directly or through advice to other sections of the Establishment. Both hardware and software have proved amenable but understandably the techniques of software promotion have advanced the less rapidly. There is need for development here not least with the government policy-maker "market" in mind.

Sixth, development groups. These comprise mixed teams of architects, engineers, surveyors, and administrators, who work within an organization to develop solutions to the problems affecting the design and construction of the type of building for which the organization is responsible. They are included in this section because of their importance in dissemination of research results, although their activities extend beyond this.

Such groups are a feature of government departments in the United Kingdom with building responsibilities. In the Department of Education and Science, for example, new layouts of schools have been developed which suit modern educational theories and new methods of construction devised which offer economies in time and money. Typically the development includes a demonstration scheme in which, say, a school is built according to the prescribed methods. The results of these developments are published reports and are given expression in circulars and other communications from central and local government.

Seventh, mobility of technologists. Though not a major factor in determining mobility, technology transfer undoubtedly benefits from it. Boundaries necessarily exist between one institution and another. These boundaries constitute barriers which have to be penetrated if technology transfer is to be effective (the "not invented here" syndrome is well known). For this reason the movement of people carrying knowledge with them in their heads in changing employment from one organization to another can be a very effective method of technology transfer. It is believed by some to account for a good deal of the success which the United States has had in converting ideas into practice. The scope in the building industry would seem however to be less than in certain other industries particularly those which are small and rapidly growing. This is evident when one considers the amount of mobility needed to affect directly the enormous number of building firms for example. In indirect terms, however, through transfer of attitudes to people in key positions, the influence, though difficult to quantify, may be much greater.

Discussion

The foregoing analysis suggests that the building industry, in common with many other traditional industries, has moved in the last 50 years in such a way as to call for a more systematically applied marketing approach to the selection of research problems and application of the results. Despite this approach and despite the considerable increase in the amount of effort devoted to dissemination and allied activities, it is felt that research results are still not being applied as effectively as they might be. Many potential users find that they are receiving too much information, a good deal of it insufficiently relevant to their problems, or only applied with difficulty. Many are not aware of the contribution existing research results could make to the solution of their problems.

Various ways of improving the situation have been suggested. Diversion of resources towards education has been proposed, the aim being to create the necessary infrastructure within the user organizations to enable them to develop the ability to receive and more particularly to adapt to technological innovation. Still further increase in dissemination activities at the expense

of research has been called for, in particular greater involvement of research
specialists in dissemination and increased co-operation between research and
application specialists. It has been suggested that more effort should be
devoted to identification of application possibilities early in the course of
the research and that more effort should be devoted to determining the best
means of dissemination (e.g. report, seminar, film, regulation, etc.) appropriate to any given results. Diversion of effort from research to the adaptation of research results to specific needs has been suggested. All these
courses involve a proportionate decrease in research effort and are therefore
to be approached with special caution.

Other suggestions include an increased concentration on selective communication of research results (to users likely to take the lead and to inspire
others); a clearer definition of responsibilities for production and utilization of research results; and a review of the effectiveness of computerized
information storage and retrieval – this last on the grounds that such systems
cannot easily provide critical appraisal of the value of the information they
handle.

The value of any of these solutions or palliatives will vary from one country
to another, but two generalizations can be made: there is a need for improvement; and we are not in a good position to evaluate the likely benefits to be
derived from the changes which are being suggested.

Conclusion

Perhaps significant improvement will be achieved only when there is better
understanding of the processes involved in the goal setting/research/applica-
tion cycle. This calls for a more advanced model, or should one say subtle
view, of the research/application process, and above all for knowledge of the
ways in which decision-makers currently become aware of and react to technological information. Given this understanding, it should be possible to establish
more rationally the roles of educational establishments, national data banks
and non-specialist advisory centres; targets for research might be pinpointed
with greater precision; marketing would be more soundly based; decisions
about the best mix of dissemination methods in particular instances would be
made more objectively; and the least productive activities would be elimi-
nated. New forms of co-operation might be involved to give improved feedback from user to researcher as well as better dissemination; there should
be increasingly effective penetration by the researcher himself into the
activities of the users and into the growing number of regulatory, standard-
producing, evaluation and approval organizations which are coming to exist
at the interface between the innovator and the user; and users might gain
a better understanding of the research process and so be able to influence it
more effectively.

Studies of this sort constitute part of a range of activities which includes
the methodology of cost/benefit analysis and forecasting, all aiming to
improve the overall efficiency of the research/application system. Participants in the seminar might usefully discuss the value of further studies of
the technology transfer process, which seems to have had less attention than
research management has had, although the issues are no less complex and this
subject is just as important.

It is true that the "applied research industry", being relatively small and
having a very diversified product, cannot easily afford the resources to
carry out such studies in depth. Moreover, selection, application, and studies

of the principles on which they are based are not yet generally regarded as activities carrying the same status as does technological research. These limitations should be regarded, however, not as insuperable obstacles but as impediments to be overcome.

ACKNOWLEDGEMENTS

The author wishes to acknowledge the source of some of the principles listed in the section Principles of Technology Transfer. The first four propositions and the seventh and eighth are paraphrased from 'Transfer of Technology in the United Kingdom', a memorandum submitted by Dr. Ron Johnston, Department of Liberal Studies in Science, University of Manchester, to the Science Sub-Committee of the Select Committee of the House of Commons on Science and Technology, Session 1975/76.

He also wishes to express his thanks to Mr. Reiners, Director of Research Policy, Departments of the Environment and Transport, and to his colleagues in the Building Research Establishment, especially Mr. W. Ransom, for the helpful comments and assistance received in preparation of the paper.

ANNEX

United Kingdom Building Research Organizations (1)
Research related to building is currently carried out in government research
establishments (mostly in the Building Research Establishment), in the universities and in other centres of higher education (applied research as well as
basic), in the larger firms, and in a number of research associations which
are funded co-operatively by industry mostly with government support. If the
definition of research is broadened to include development, certain government
agencies and local authorities should be included.

United Kingdom Users and Their Research Needs (2)
The architect works up a client's broad requirements into a detailed design
and specification, obtains planning and by-law approval, usually obtains
competitive quotations from contractors (depending upon the nature of the
contractual procedures used), supervises progress and issues certificates for
payments. He wishes to obtain good value for money spent, and for this reason
is interested in research results, preferably in the form of design guides and
specifications. Few architectural practices can provide the effort needed to
translate results into this form, although it is possible to a certain extent
in architects' departments in central government and in some large local
authorities. Many of the forms of communication described in this paper seek
therefore to assist this translation of knowledge. There often remains a gap
however which is a restraint on application.

There is a need also for research specifically into architectural practice
itself, and concomitant information needs (this sort of research is not
strongly based but is growing, particularly in the universities).

The structural engineer prepares structural drawings and advises the architect
on related implications. Naturally he is mainly concerned with research into
structural engineering and materials behaviour and, on the whole, is well
served by research bodies. The gap between research results and their application is thus narrower though there is still a need for simple design guides.
Effort to prepare these can be found in-house in the larger firms of consultants. (There are strong bases of research in structural engineering in
government research establishments and the universities).

The building contractor undertakes to construct in accordance with the
contract documents usually within a specific period of time. He is concerned
particularly with construction processes including the use of plant. The
largest firms have their own research and development branches and are
receptive to research. However, the great majority do not have professional
staff able to digest and adapt research results and the structure of the
building industry in general hinders the application of research; for when
builders construct to a specification, there is little incentive for them to
be concerned particularly with research activities - let alone engage in them.
In general there is a lack of research aimed at their principal interests
which are to build to a specification as quickly and cheaply as possible.

Most contractors feel that to engage directly in research would only result in benefits to the industry as a whole and would not provide a reasonable competitive edge to their own firm. The Construction Industry Research and Information Association (CIRIA) provides a general research service to contractors but most members are civil engineering firms rather than building contractors.

The contractor may sub-contract many parts of the whole construction process. Few specialist sub-contractors have facilities, expertise or even incentive to use research results and in general the comments made above on the main building contractor apply here.

The manufacturers of components and materials engage in much development and innovation with some underlying research activity. Over the years the developments in materials, components (and plant) have had a major influence in both design and the construction processes. The larger firms are able to benefit from background research and there is much transfer of technology from other industries. Indeed innovation often outpaces necessary basic studies.

The Department of the Environment is responsible for general housing and planning policies, for the drafting and introduction of national building regulations, and for policies related to construction generally. The Department is responsible also for a large public building programme.

The research base is provided principally by the Building Research Establishment and some Headquarters directorates. There is close contact between policy directorates and researchers through a committee structure which serves to advise on research needs. Public building being on a larger scale, the government organization responsible, the Property Services Agency of the Department of the Environment, has been able to set up services which advise and carry out a certain amount of development work, for the benefit primarily of the public sector. Knowledge of research results is rapid but the administrative issues involved are usually complex and may delay or even prevent their application.

Local authorities are responsible generally for the implementation of specific housing and planning decisions and also for the enforcement of building control. Though some of these authorities, notably the Greater London Council, have scientific branches, few have strong internal facilities for either undertaking research or translating the results of others. This can impose a limitation on the application of results.

The British Standards Institution and the Agrément Board are the main organizations concerned with standards and other forms of assessment and certification. Both bodies have close contact with both researchers and testing authorities and they have access to technical expertise sufficient to minimize problems of interpretation.

United Kingdom Building Regulations and Specifications (3)
The national building regulations are concerned with securing the health, safety, welfare and convenience of persons in or about buildings, with the conservation of fuel and power and with the prevention of waste, misuse and contamination of water. They are phrased firstly to state an overall requirement in rather general terms but usually also they refer to "deemed to satisfy" provisions. Compliance with the technical content of these provisions ensures compliance with the regulations. The "deemed to satisfy" clauses generally refer to British Standard Codes of Practice, which represent

a standard of good practice, and to standards. Research results incorporated into these standards, codes and regulations ensure their wide adoption and this is a major way of introducing research results into normal practice. The timescale for introduction, however, is generally long; the requirements in British Standards can, too, tend towards those capable of achievement by the generality of the associated parts of the industry.

The need to encourage innovation while still providing adequate safeguards of quality has led in the United Kingdom and elsewhere to other schemes of specification to supplement these national standards. The Agrément Board sponsored by the Department of the Environment assesses how new products are likely to behave in service over the years. The assessments are published as Agrément Certificates containing information to enable products to be used correctly and to prevent costly and dangerous failures. Very close contact is maintained between the Board and research organizations in particular with the Building Research Establishment with which organization there are both formal and informal links and on whose site the Board has established testing and research facilities. This contact enables rapid assimilation of the consequences of research results into the clauses of the Certificates and thus into general practice.

While still needing to conform to the overall national regulations individual organizations may of course introduce their own specifications. If such bodies are concerned with major building activities such as the Greater London Council or the Property Services Agency, then the effect of these specifications can be widespread. Also they can usually be brought into effect and revised more readily than national standards. These specifications may take a number of forms and relate to major buildings, to specialist procedures, to maintenance and so on. Research results can be and are incorporated into them quickly though an interpretative phase is often needed between research and such application. When those drafting specifications serve as "customers" for research on committees concerned with the formulation of research needs – as happens in the Department of the Environment – then application is greatly assisted.

United Kingdom Building Research Establishment Application Section (4)
The operation hinges upon identification of a "target audience". The categories of potential user and beneficiary, not necessarily identical, are listed along with other interests which directly or indirectly could affect or influence adoption of the technology in question. The separate components of the overall target audience are carefully identified and means of communication chosen suitable to each. Following this, a synchronized application campaign is mounted in which both research workers and specialists in various fields of communications take a part. As originator of the results the research worker plays a vital role in formulation and planning of the campaign which should begin, if not at the initiation of the research, as soon as positive results are starting to emerge. Both hardware and software subjects have been handled, results not infrequently combining hardware and software in significant proportions, for instance a new material and the process of making it or a building system combining special plant, building designs and erection methods.

Because many products of research which have been hailed as technological breakthroughs either never reach the market or, worse, become embarrassing failures, concern has frequently been voiced about the existence of an "application gap" between research and industry. Among the many reasons for this "gap" must be cited inadequate attention on the part of the researcher to the likely reactions of a commercial innovator who is invited to exploit a technological advance which is offered to him. He has to be convinced that the development is really practicable and that the product is likely to be more saleable than existing products. He also has to satisfy himself about many questions such as the cost and timescale of development, probable levels of demand and whether the demand exists or will have to be cultivated, production costs, compatibility of the product with the production skills and market outlets at his disposal, capital investment, competition from other firms and products, patent protection and the rate of technical evolution in the field concerned which dictates the life of the market for the product. It is not suggested that the research organization can supply answers to all his questions, but before an approach is made to a potential innovator, the research side should have given considerable thought to them and to ways in which it can co-operate with the innovator in securing answers to his questions. Finally it may be necessary to call in a specialist agency such as the National Research Development Corporation to clinch the arrangements.

With "software" applications the identification of target audience and selection of appropriate communication methods is similar to that for "hardware". Thereafter the implications of applying the results need to be thought through in co-operation with the possible user, e.g. the policy maker, generally a more difficult task than with "hardware" but just as important.

The marketing which has been described is of course only part of the whole. Identification of research goals through researcher/user consultation is an important first stage which is covered by Subject A of this seminar.

INTERNATIONAL COLLABORATION (PART I)

ACTIVITIES OF THE INTERNATIONAL COUNCIL FOR BUILDING RESEARCH, STUDIES AND DOCUMENTATION (CIB)

J.B. Dick, President of the CIB

J.B. Dick, President of the CIB

INTRODUCTION

In 1949 the International Council for Building Documentation, (CIDB), was created following the initiative of the United Nations Economic Commission for Europe (ECE) in Geneva. The aim was to encourage co-operation at non-governmental level with regard to scientific and technical work undertaken to support governmental policies. This activity on building information and documentation was subsequently extended in 1953 to form the International Council for Building Research, Studies and Documentation, (CIB). This paper is being prepared on behalf of CIB in response to an invitation from the organizing committee for the ECE Seminar on Building Research Policies to report on the stage of development reached after twenty-five years and from its experience and knowledge to contribute on international aspects of building research policies.

The paper outlines the main objectives of CIB, and goes on to consider how successful CIB has been in reaching its main objectives, reviewing not only the successes achieved, but also various problems which have been encountered; it also discusses possible developments in the future particularly in the context of governmental building research policies.

As a basis for reviewing progress in CIB it is as well to start by setting down the main purpose of CIB as stated in one of the Articles of its Constitution:

"Purpose
The purpose of CIB is to encourage, facilitate and develop international co-operation in building, housing and planning research, studies and documentation, covering not only the technical but also the economic and social aspects of building and the related environment. CIB will use its best endeavours, within the limits of its competence, to promote progress in these fields by improving quality, reducing costs and increasing productivity".

Although in the present context this can be regarded as the most important objective, it is also worthwhile mentioning two further Articles which are relevant to an overall review:

"International co-operation
CIB shall promote, for international benefit, the co-ordination and co-operation of existing international and national organizations, within the limits of its competence".

55

"United Nations

CIB shall collaborate with the United Nations through those branches
of its activity that are concerned with intergovernmental co-operation in the fields of building, housing and planning. In effecting
this liaison, CIB shall adhere to the United Nations as a Non-
Governmental Organization in an appropriate category".

and these aspects will also be covered in the course of the discussion.

First of all a few words about the organization and methods of working adopted
in CIB. The governing body in which the authority of CIB is vested is the
General Assembly composed of representatives of full members; this body meets
at least every three years and appoints a Board to take charge of current
management. In turn, a Programme Committee and an Administrative Committee
are appointed to which are delegated various ongoing detailed responsibilities.
These activities and the needs of the 200 members are served by a small General
Secretariat in Rotterdam, the policy being that the General Secretariat should
deal mainly with the overall administration and that the scientific and technical development of CIB work should stem from the efforts of the members
themselves. In parenthesis it may be mentioned that the possibility of establishing a scientific secretariat which could provide a corresponding leadership in research collaboration has been examined, but it is clearly much more
effective to utilize the wide range of knowledge and expertise which members
have, rather than attempt to provide central expertise across the spectrum of
subjects of interest: the expenditure involved would be at least an order of
magnitude higher than at present.

INTERNATIONAL COLLABORATION IN RESEARCH

The main work of CIB is carried out in a series of Working Commissions and
Steering Groups (a current list is appended). Each of these has a Co-ordinator, who is responsible for developing work, and the ongoing and proposed new
activities are reviewed regularly by the Programme Committee.

The Steering Groups have the task of arranging and developing symposia on their
subjects as thought to be required: in practice this usually implies meetings
at intervals of some two or three years.

The Working Commissions, on the other hand, show more variation in their
methods of operation and important developments in their mode of working have
taken place over the years. In its simplest form, a Commission may, by corres-
pondence or by arrangement of meetings, provide an opportunity for research
workers engaged on common subjects to exchange views on the problems involved,
on research programmes aimed at solving these problems, and on the results
achieved: research effort on the whole is spread thinly in the different
countries and in some specialist subjects the most effective criticism may
well come from those working in the same field in other countries. In this
way participation in a Commission may help an individual research worker to
reach more effectively his own objective which is often essentially local or
national in character. As well as this direct benefit, there can be a further
important gain in that common approaches and interpretations inevitably become
more widely accepted and informally co-ordinated. In turn, when the research
workers concerned are asked to contribute through their national organizations
to some international activities, they will do this against the background of
the CIB work. In other words, the development of a common research base can
greatly facilitate subsequent developments in intergovernmental and international standardizing organizations.

Increasingly within CIB Commissions more positive approaches to securing
further benefits have been developed. The problems in which research workers
are engaged in different countries may well have common elements, and although
from a local or national point of view, it may be necessary to have available
for local application, an expertise based on research, there is no need for
undue overlapping of effort. Therefore in a number of Commissions, the development of more direct collaboration has been encouraged with the definition
of an agreed goal and a subsequent programme of work allocated to various
members and to be completed within an agreed time limit. Individual members
with responsibilities in their own countries consistent with the agreed objectives can readily undertake the corresponding commitments; and of course
this pattern of working can, as already outlined, at a later stage have more
indirect benefits in subsequent participation in international activities.

The CIB has also been attempting to make a more direct contribution to the
activities of intergovernmental and international standardizing organizations.
In 1972 the then President, following discussions within CIB, circulated the
Co-ordinators of the various Commissions encouraging them to examine their
programmes and consider whether they could direct their work to provide a
contribution to the developing momentum towards the harmonization of regulations and standards. CIB believes that as well as providing what may be
called an international research base which can contribute indirectly through
national inputs into the international arena, that it is important to develop
this more direct contribution, and some success can certainly be claimed over
the years. There are, however, certain difficulties in pressing this development which might well profit by discussion at the seminar. A key difference
in this activity is that research workers in the various institutes, enterprises or universities may not be able to obtain explicit support for such
international activities, their brief often being limited to a more local or
national activity. On the other hand, if the international requirement is
consistent with a national one, there need be no difficulty. As explained
earlier, CIB has no central scientific secretariat which can be allocated to
such work, and we must rely on the contribution of members, and they in turn
must have sponsorship for the work required. Thus CIB would suggest that if
this development is to be encouraged, this implies that those who agree on
specific needs for intergovernmental agreement or international standardization and wish a subsequent contribution from a non-governmental organization,
such as CIB, should recognize that the required resources must be made available possibly as part of the national contribution.

Another problem in this area arises from the vastness of the field which is
potentially of interest, and clearly it is of considerable help to obtain
international agreement on the subjects to be given priority. Here the views
formulated through ECE and ISO are most helpful.

However, there is another aspect which also has to be considered and that is
whether there is sufficient knowledge about the subject concerned to envisage
practical recommendations, even after some further research, in say the next
year or so. For example, there is concern about the toxic effects of combus-
tion of some of the newer materials in building, but although one or two
countries have introduced some controls, in others there is thought to be
insufficient knowledge and on the research side there is a recognized need for
substantial further work. This example illustrates a common dilemma: in
theory it would appear that **where** there are in fact no national regulations,
it might be easiest to develop international recommendations; but on the
other hand, the available knowledge may just be inadequate for their formula-

tion if required. Reviewing the work of the CIB Commissions certainly illustrates the variation between the states of knowledge in the different subjects.
In some, one can assess that a positive contribution could well be forthcoming based on existing knowledge or possibly with that knowledge supplemented by some limited research; but in others, the path of development is not
so clear and longer term research and application will certainly be required.
Thus as well as considering priorities of needs, it is essential that the
feasibility of, for example, the development of appropriate standards be
critically examined – otherwise we may well finish with inadequate recommendations becoming enshrined.

From the CIB point of view, there is clearly a need to ensure that any commitments undertaken can be completed satisfactorily within the agreed time. This
requires that there be close consultation between those responsible for final
decisions or priorities and those responsible in CIB. In fact it should be
recognized that such a dialogue on a particular subject could be initiated by
either side and could be concerned with either short-term work or with longer
term research. But whether the proposals initiate on the CIB side or say
within ECE, it is important once again to stress, as has been discussed above,
the need to ensure that the resources required are available for the agreed
programme.

The collaborative work within the Commissions may well involve a considerable
number of research workers, but CIB also provides a forum for encouraging
direct collaboration between, say, two or three research institutes. A range
of possible subjects has been discussed, and from this several bilateral and
trilateral collaborative arrangements have been made. Collaboration takes a
number of forms: two institutes may agree to undertake complementary programmes with each specializing in a different area but maintaining sufficient
co-ordination to ensure that results can be readily transferred and will be
in a form relevant to the other's interests; in other cases, it may be a
matter of arranging consistent data collection and analysis so that comparison
of results in different countries may readily be compared and assessed – this
is particularly valuable in, for example, studies of human response to noise.

Some direct collaboration between research institutes can of course also be
set up as part of an agreement between two governments to develop a programme
of scientific and technological collaboration and there are many recent
examples. The main difference between these arrangements and those initiated
within CIB is that the collaboration is recognized at governmental level in
the countries concerned rather than simply being a private agreement between
institutes each concerned with its own objectives.

A further step in the development of collaboration in the CIB context would be
for, say, two institutes to agree on a fully joint programme when resources
would be pooled under a single (or possibly a shared) leadership. This
appears to be much more difficult within the present framework of largely
independent programmes whether sponsored by national governments or enterprises or in the university sector. In some other areas of science and technology, the development of such joint research has been a notable feature of
at least the last two decades; in a number of cases the driving force has
been the initial cost of the sophisticated equipment required and also the
subsequent cost of experiment and development. With this possible need in
mind, it was arranged in CIB some six years ago to prepare an inventory of the
equipment and facilities in the laboratories of member institutes. This,
however, has not led to joint work, or so far as is known, to arrangements to

use another institute's facilities to meet the needs of a particular programme
in another country. In CIB we have envisaged that there are occasions when
the research needs of one institute might well be met by a research programme
undertaken by another institute in another country, making use not only of
appropriate laboratory equipment but also of the specialized knowledge and
expertise of research staff. But many difficulties exist, such as foreign
exchange problems and local priorities, and this is perhaps a development for
the future. As already illustrated by the discussion of the problems which
can occur when Commissions aim at international objectives, at present although
much progress has been made in building research in developing increased collaboration and communication between research workers, there are still many
challenges to be met in attempting a fuller international integration where
this could be profitable.

In this context it is relevant to mention here a CIB initiative which is
currently being explored. Many members feel that CIB should try to make a
larger contribution to solving problems encountered in developing countries.
As part of this and as an explicit follow-up to Habitat, a seminar on "Building Research and its Application in Developing Countries" was held in
New Delhi in March 1977. But it is hoped that it will be possible to supplement this one-off event by a more continuous activity, and members are being
asked whether they could make available resources, whether of finance, research
effort or other services to support a consolidated effort by CIB. The hope is
that sufficient resources might be forthcoming to enable CIB to set up a focal
point in, say, one of the institutes which in turn would co-ordinate the CIB
approach utilizing any further resources which members could offer. This
approach is perhaps rather an exceptional one and it is not yet clear what
success will be achieved. It does, however, illustrate that many methods of
increasing the CIB contribution generally are being explored, and of course
is particularly relevant in the present context in that it interacts with
government policies towards the support of research in developing countries.

The CIB encourages all its members to participate in the range of activities
outlined above. The world-wide membership and the geographical distances
between interested research institutes present difficulties in establishing
and maintaining the desirable links, and CIB has tried and is still trying a
variety of approaches to solve the problems involved. For example, members
unable to attend meetings of Working Commissions become corresponding members.
Regional activities are being encouraged in which a member organizes a "workshop" on the subject of a CIB Working Commission or Symposium which members
in his region can attend. Instead of a one-off "workshop" a more continuous
working group can be set up regionally as a counterpart commission. And
finally although most of the Commissions are essentially European-based, CIB
is encouraging a number of Commissions centred outside Europe. The same
applies to seminars or symposia and that to be held in New Delhi on Building
Research and its Application in Developing Countries is an important example.
Overall then, CIB has developed a policy of encouraging regional activities,
the subjects being selected in principle by the local CIB members; this
approach appears preferable to one which involves setting up permanent regional
organizations of CIB. This extension of CIB activities implies a need for
closer liaison with other regional United Nations Commissions: CIB and ECE
have maintained close links over the years, but although CIB has had various
contacts with other United Nations Commissions, it would appear that such
relationships could well be developed. ECE could perhaps help by conveying
its positive experience with CIB to the other regional organizations.

SOME CIB CONTRIBUTIONS

As already mentioned, part of the benefit arising from CIB activities accrues
to the individual research worker who participates and this is not readily
quantified. There are of course various reports which emerge from the ongoing work within CIB and appear in national and international scientific and
technical journals, but the overall contribution to international development
is not necessarily simply measured by these. For example, although Working
Commission W24 "Dimensional and Modular Co-ordination" has over the years
published several reports, perhaps its most important role has been to provide
the central forum for international discussion of a subject which is fundamental in any move towards greater harmonization of building products.

The CIB, however, has over the years sponsored a series of publications as
official reports on work undertaken by Working Commissions or as Proceedings
of Symposia, and in the present context it is worthwhile listing some of these
as being indicative of part of the contribution which has been made. The
titles given below have been selected because of their bearing on subjects of
interest to ECE; a full list of publications is available from the CIB Secretariat. Generally the reports from Working Commissions (WC) are concerned
with specific work undertaken by the Commissions and represent agreed views
and recommendations by members which have been accepted by CIB; the reports
on Symposia (S) bring together contributions on a particular subject from
many countries covering the latest research results and providing a review of
the state of knowledge.

Information Flow   – Information flow in the building
                                          process: classification and coding
                                          for computer use. (S 1968)

                                        – Some problems of information flow in
                                          the building process. (S 1970)

Classification   – Abridged Building Classification for
                                          Architects, Builders and Civil Engi-
                                          neers (1965)

                                        – The SfB System (WC 1973)

                                        – CIB Master Lists for Structuring docu-
                                          ments (WC 1972)

                                        – Guide to the Use of SfB (WC In the
                                          Press)

Performance   – Performance Concept in Buildings.
                                          Proceedings of Joint RILEM/ASTM/CIB
                                          Symposium 1972.

                                        – The Performance Concept and its Termi-
                                          nology (WC 1975)

Economics   – Methodology of Cost Comparisons (WC 1972)

                                        – Assessing the Economics of Building
                                          (S 1974)

Dimensions   – Geometry of Joints (WC 1976)

Tolerances and Accuracy	– Tolerances and Accuracy in Buildings Joint CIB/FIG (S 1971)
	– A Checklist on Tolerances (WC 1974)
	– Measuring Practice on the Building Site Joint CIB/FIG (WC 1975)
Climatology	– Climatology and Building (S 1970)
	– Survey of Meteorological Information for Architecture and Building (WC 1972)
	– Teaching the Teacher (S 1972)
	– The Analysis of Climatological Data for the Building Industry (WC In the Press)
Heat and Moisture	– Moisture Problems in Building RILEM/CIB (S 1965)
	– Weathertight Joints for Walls (S 1967)
	– Thermal Comfort and Moderate Heat Stress (S 1972)
	– Moisture in Buildings RILEM/CIB (S 1974)
	– Energy Conservation in the Built Environment (S 1976)
Fire	– Fully Developed Fires in Single Compartments (WC 1972)
Structures	– Bearing Walls (S 1969)
	– On Methods of Load Calculation (WC 19)
Building types	– Low-Rise Lightweight Constructions (S 1971)
	– Tall Buildings (S 1971)
	– Box Unit Constructions (S 1973)
	– Industrial Buildings (S 1973)

Added to the above are of course the publications arising from the Triennial Congress which provide regular broad reviews of the development of building research over the years. The main themes of the Congresses held so far are given below:

    Building Research and Documentation 1959
    Innovation in Building 1962
    Towards Industrialized Building 1965
    Building – Cost and Quality 1968
    Research into Practice: The Challenge of Application 1971
    The Impact of Research on the Built Environment 1974

Finally it is perhaps worth noting some current subjects in the programme of the Working Party on the Building Industry where CIB activities are making a contribution:

  (i)   Energy Conservation
  (ii)   Systems of Building Regulations
 (iii)   Formulation of Requirement levels in Functional terms
  (iv)   Building Climatology
   (v)   Principles for Load Bearing Structures
  (vi)   Fire Protection Requirements for Residential Buildings
 (vii)   Harmonization in relation to Human Requirements in Buildings
(viii)   Regulations for Designing Timber Structures

THE COVERAGE OF RESEARCH IN CIB

Over the years the general pattern of the subjects of building research has
changed. In the early years of CIB the main emphasis was related to the application of the physical sciences in building but many institutes have increasingly developed research on problems related to social, economic and operational problems of building. This shift has been, of course, reflected in
the developments in setting up (and terminating) Working Commissions and also
recent symposia. It is perhaps as well to give here some indication of various
probes which are now being made and which may come to fruition in the near
future.

There are two main studies being made at present. The first of these is
concerned with establishing the interest of member institutes in CIB in the
urban planning field. A number of institutes are working in this field, particularly on problems related to architectural planning but also on the related engineering services in towns and cities. The question is whether there
is sufficient on-going activity to justify some form of collaborative work.
In many cases the work is at an early stage, but it is of course at this stage
that collaborative arrangements may be most effective. The ECE secretariat is
being kept informed of these developments.

Secondly, CIB is examining possible further collaborative work in the field of
housing and the community. Again many institutes are working on different
aspects of housing but at present, apart from a Commission dealing with low-
cost housing in developing countries, CIB has not co-ordinated effort in this
field. It has already been agreed to set up a Working Commission concerned
with Housing Sociology which will supplement an existing Commission dealing
with Human Requirements, but will be concerned not only with the response to
the physical environment but also with social needs. Clearly, further initiatives by CIB in this field may well have a contribution to make at a later
stage back to ECE.

Although in some institutes there has been some shift of resources from the
technological aspects to social and economic aspects, in general in past years
it can be said that building research has expanded as a whole. What has been
happening is that the increase in the social, economic and operational research
has been notably larger than that on the technological side.

INFORMATION ACTIVITIES OF CIB

An important part of the work of CIB is the provision of information on
building research to its members and to the broader international community.
The output from the Working Commissions and Steering Groups has already been
discussed and in this section, some of the other main activities are outlined.

For a research worker to be fully effective he needs to know not only the

important research reports in his area but also to be familiar with the ongoing research and even the planned research in that area. In CIB we have
explored how far we can go in filling gaps in this network. It has proved
difficult to systematize plans for future research; in most countries the
commitments for the future are subject to considerable discussion and it is
difficult to draw up even tentative plans which might be useful in providing
prior notice. Rather we have concentrated on trying to ensure that, when
research programmes have been decided, knowledge about these should be promul-
gated freely. Several Working Commissions as part of their activities produce
regular detailed reviews of current research, and on a more general level, a
group of member institutes provide information about their programmes to the
central secretariat and direct to other participating members. Initially this
system was based on preparation of special research project cards but some
members found this too difficult and now all members are invited to make
available copies of their own research programmes in the form drawn up for
their own use to other institutes who are prepared to engage in bilateral
exchanges of programmes and can cope with the language concerned. This is
supplemented by a regular listing in the CIB Newsletter of all research
programmes received at the CIB Secretariat provided they are in one of the
more accessible languages. As an experiment a computerized index to the
research programmes of the participating institutes has just been prepared.
This will be given a trial run to see if it successfully provides the access
required to the set of programmes concerned.

Another area in which international collaboration has been sought is in the
preparation of abstracts. Not all institutes prepare abstracts but a number
do and it was thought that there was no need to duplicate. In practice only
a limited success can be claimed here.

It is worth mentioning here CIB experience in relation to publication of an
international journal. In 1968 it was decided to sponsor an international
magazine which it was thought could eventually be a commercial success without
financial support from CIB, but in the event the journal now produced does
absorb some 10 per cent of the income of CIB. This amount has been allocated
because CIB considers that the promulgation of news of its activities is essential if it is to play its full part in developing building research and documentation.

As well as these continuing information activities, a number of specific
initiatives have been undertaken. Some have already been mentioned in the
course of the paper; others are included in the overall summary given below:

Research Programmes	Exchange of research programmes of participating CIB institutes
	Periodic review of research on heating and ventilation
	Periodic review of research on fire
Directories	Directory of Facilities for Developing Countries (1965)
	Directory of Building Research, Informa-tion and Development Organizations (1971)
	International Catalogue of Films on Building, Architecture and Physical Planning (1972)

Register of Specialized Equipment in
use in Building Research Organizations
(1971)

Periodical   Building Research and Practice (Bi-
                                        monthly)

Newsletter   CIB Newsletter (Bi-monthly)

COLLABORATION WITH OTHER INTERNATIONAL ORGANIZATIONS

Part of the brief for CIB already mentioned is to promote the co-ordination
and co-operation of existing international and national organizations. It is
sometimes said that the multiplicity of non-governmental organizations in the
field of building research presents a very complex picture. To the outsider
this may be the case. There is of course a danger that the various independent organizations will act in an unco-ordinated way with undue overlap or
conflicting activities. But many of those involved are very conscious of
this, and having established international collaboration in their subjects,
are keen to collaborate with other bodies in related fields. On the other
hand, we would stress that there seems to be no need for further international
organizations in the general field.

To a large extent the contacts between the various existing bodies are informal
but regular exchanges have also been developed, e.g. CIB and RILEM, which deal
with a range of related subjects, have cross-representation on their programming committees. In the broader building and civil engineering field, a
special annual meeting of a Liaison Committee reviews the work carried out
and planned in seven specialist bodies; this is perhaps a pattern which
could be usefully established in other limited fields. Such arrangements for
co-ordination should not, however, get too rigid or complex. The test is
whether they can help the various members to improve efficiency in their own
tasks in their own countries or alternatively help the individual organization
in developing its own work to make the maximum contribution internationally.
An important development in the approach on this Liaison Committee has been to
agree that certain organizations should take the lead in developing work on
subjects of common interest.

For example, it has been agreed by the non-governmental organizations concerned
that CIB through its Working Commission in Fire should take the lead in examining the technical basis for Fire Codes relating to different materials and
in developing internationally agreed statements at the research level on the
principles of fire safety. This work is being done in collaboration with the
non-governmental organizations specializing in different materials – steel,
wood, concrete, pre-stressed concrete, etc., and clearly can provide the
basis of a most useful contribution to ISO and ECE in this field.

A further example is in the structural field, where CEB, although normally
only dealing with concrete is taking the lead on structural safety and providing a focus for integrating work being done on other materials – CIB has
Working Commissions dealing with structural aspects of timber and masonry and
is contributing in relation to these materials.

These examples of the type of arrangements being agreed between non-governmental organizations may well provide useful prototypes for further development
of collaboration, not only in the field covered by the present Liaison Committee.

The recognition of a 'lead' organization with a responsibility for initiation and development of an integrated, co-ordinated approach is regarded by CIB as being an important and appropriate step forward in increasing international collaboration.

SUMMARY AND CONCLUSIONS

The paper has covered many aspects of CIB activities and international collaboration in building research and documentation. To assist in focusing discussion at the seminar it is probably helpful to summarize some of the main points made:

Many problems in building research are common to many countries. CIB has had considerable success in assisting individual research workers to attain the objectives of their own work.

In turn, research workers in different countries contributing towards the work of intergovernmental and international standardizing bodies have drawn on the international research base established by CIB, and this indirect contribution from CIB has greatly facilitated progress.

In some areas where national objectives are consistent with international ones, it has been possible for CIB to undertake commitments to international bodies and thus to make direct contributions to international work.

CIB would be glad to develop such contributions and would stress the need, for those participating at official level in the statement of international requirements, to provide support to CIB and other non-governmental organizations by appropriate allocation of resources, in particular from their own countries.

There is a need for a continuing review of priorities for international work. Assessment of priorities should take into account, not only the inherent importance of subjects but also the relevant state of knowledge. Some subjects may require only a review of existing knowledge and an ordering of such information in a suitable form; for others it may be that fairly long-term research is required to provide the necessary understanding.

It follows that proposals for international work could be initiated either at intergovernmental level or on the research side in one of the non-governmental organizations and should then be examined jointly. The ECE has already of course initiated discussions with CIB on some of its specific agreed needs; it is considered that CIB could also take the initiative in proposing programmes of research particularly to meet rather longer term needs in certain areas of interest.

The CIB would recommend to governments that they should support the development of more direct collaboration between research institutes in different countries where this appears to be of benefit to the parties concerned.

It is suggested that liaison between the main existing non-govern-

mental organizations is developing satisfactorily and is leading
to a closer integration of effort. It is emphasized, however, that
further multiplicity of non-governmental organizations seems
undesirable.

CIB has maintained and developed close working links with ECE. It
is suggested that ECE could encourage other regional organizations
of the United Nations to develop their links with CIB.

LIST OF WORKING COMMISSIONS

Joint Commissions:

W9	Structural safety

CIB Commissions:

S4	Climatology and building
W6	Collection climatological data for the building industry
W8	Modification by buildings
W14	Fire
S17	Heating and climatization
W18	Timber structures
W19	Large concrete elements
W23	Structural requirements
W23A	Load bearing walls
W24	Modular co-ordination - IMG
W29	Concrete surface finishes
W40	Heat and moisture transfer
S41	Tall buildings
W45	Human requirements
W49	Tolerances
W51	Acoustics
W52	Building information and its computer application
W53	Forecasting methods
W54	Selection research projects
W55	Building economics
S56	Lightweight constructions
W57	Managers of documentation units
W60	Performance concept
W61	Joints in exterior walls
W62	Water supply and drainage
W63	Low cost housing
TS64	Municipal engineering
W65	Organization of construction
S66	Industrial buildings
W67	Energy conservation
TW68	Environmental design in tropics
W69	Housing sociology

INTERNATIONAL COLLABORATION: (PART II)

REVIEW OF EXISTING ARRANGEMENTS* **

Introductory report prepared by the ECE secretariat

INTRODUCTION

More than half of all investments in ECE countries take the form of construction works. Most of what is constructed, modernized and maintained is directly or indirectly influenced by government decisions through building regulations, stipulations for financial aid and subsidies, public financing, etc. Against this background, it is obviously of great interest to governments to ensure that economy and efficiency is achieved throughout the design and construction process, in the production, transport and handling of building materials and components and in the maintenance, modernization and operation of buildings and other construction works.

As in all other sectors of the economy, progress in the building materials and construction industries is greatly influenced by research and development work. In view of the importance of the building sector, the heavy government involvement in the production, financing and utilization of the building products and the dispersed nature of the industry, nearly all ECE governments have recognized their responsibility to ensure that adequate resources are set aside for building research and development work, that work in this field is oriented in the interests of the society and that it is organized in an effective manner.

International collaboration in the field of building research and development work may contribute significantly towards achieving economy and efficiency. Despite certain differences in the socio-economic conditions and the physical environment in the ECE region, there are major prospects for international cooperation by an exchange of research programmes and research results relating to building design, materials and construction technologies. The promotion of systematic and intensive international collaboration in building research and development work should therefore be seen as an integral and important part of building research policies in ECE countries.

ACTIVITIES OF INTERNATIONAL ORGANIZATIONS CONCERNED WITH BUILDING RESEARCH AND DEVELOPMENT WORK

Economic Commission for Europe

---

*A detailed review of the activities of the International Council for Building Research, Studies and Documentation (CIB) is contained in a paper by J.B. Dick, President of the CIB, which is included in these proceedings. The descriptive part of the present document is therefore concentrated on other international organizations active in the field of building research, development work and documentation.

**A key to the abbreviations used is provided in annex I to this paper.

The Economic Commission for Europe (ECE), through its Committee on Housing, Building and Planning, has taken an interest in building research and development work since its inception in 1947. Its first major initiative in this area resulted in the setting up, in 1950, of a new international non-governmental organization, the International Council for Building Documentation (CIDB). The purpose of that organization was to provide a link between national centres or committees for building documentation and to promote the establishment of common principles with regard to terminology, classification and methods of arranging and presenting building documentation. Next, following an ECE Conference on Building Research, a recommendation was made to governments to establish, where this did not already exist, national organizations for building research in their countries. A small ECE organizing group then established the scope and nature of international collaboration in building research, drew attention to the close links between research and documentation and concluded by recommending the setting up of a new international non-governmental body. Subsequently, after further preparatory work both by the ECE and the CIDB, the CIDB was formally transformed into the International Council for Building Research, Studies and Documentation (CIB), in 1953.

The creation of CIB was in itself considered by ECE as a major breakthrough. It also had the effect of enabling the ECE secretariat to concentrate its limited resources on key government policy issues of an economic and social character related to housing, building and physical planning. Close contacts and links of co-operation, both formal and informal, have been maintained between ECE and CIB throughout the years. ECE staff officials regularly attend the meetings of the CIB Board and the CIB Programme Committee and also contribute to and actively participate in the CIB Congresses. The co-operation between the two organizations was intensified in 1964, when the Working Party on the Building Industry of the Committee on Housing, Building and Planning was established, and took on a new dimension with the initiation, in 1973, of the ECE programme for the harmonization of the technical content of building regulations. In the Policy Statement constituting the intergovernmental basis for this work, it is stated, inter alia, that the Working Party on the Building Industry should "promote co-operation among non-governmental international organizations concerned with standardization and research activities related to building regulations; and review priorities and progress of international standardization and research activities related to regulations on building and building machinery" (ECE/HBP/7, annex II, clause G). In pursuing these objectives, co-operation has been established with several CIB Working Commissions and some forty other international organizations.

In 1970, the Committee on Housing, Building and Planning requested the Working Party on the Building Industry to initiate a study on building research policies. Following considerable preparatory work, an in-depth discussion on this subject was held by the Working Party in June 1975, on the basis of papers submitted by nine countries. It was then concluded that a special ECE seminar on building research policies should be held in 1977.

Other United Nations Agencies

The United Nations Centre for Housing, Building and Planning (UNCHBP) belongs to the Department of Economic and Social Affairs of the United Nations Secretariat. Located in New York City, the Centre carries out studies, promotes research and supervises the activities of a large number of experts assisting developing countries in the field of housing, building and planning. The Building Section of the Centre is actively interested in building research activities,

especially for the benefit of the developing countries. Assistance has already
been given to regions other than ECE with a view to encouraging existing research institutes and promoting co-operation among them.

The United Nations Industrial Development Organization (UNIDO), located in
Vienna, is a specialized agency mainly concentrating on the development of manufacturing industries (including building materials production). However, the
construction industry is also dealt with to some extent, in consultation and
co-operation with UNCHBP, ILO, FAO, and other United Nations agencies concerned.
UNIDO has aimed so far primarily at facilitating a transfer and adaptation of
production technology for the benefit of developing countries, through studies,
field visits and technical assistance projects.

The United Nations Environment Programme (UNEP) is a co-ordinating and fund-
allocating agency, located in Nairobi. "Human settlements and Habitat" has been
identified as one of UNEP's priority areas and a section of the UNEP secretariat
is dealing with problems in this field. The activities have so far concentrated
on the organization of the United Nations Conference on Human Settlements (Habitat 1976). The Conference recommended that strong emphasis in the follow-up
work should be given to regional activities and to the promotion of research
and development work within and outside the United Nations system. UNEP has
initiated a comprehensive project, the main aim of which is to establish regional networks of institutes concerned with human settlements technology. These
regional networks are then planned to be linked up into a global network.

The United Nations Educational and Scientific Organisation (UNESCO) is located
in Paris. The Conference on Security and Co-operation in Europe (Helsinki 1975)
stressed that further emphasis should be given to the promotion of scientific
and technological co-operation, including the setting up of a Scientific Forum
by UNESCO in consultation with the ECE.

Other United Nations agencies concerned with research and development in building materials and construction are the International Labour Office (ILO), located in Geneva, the Food and Agriculture Organization (FAO), located in Rome,
the World Meteorological Organization (WMO) and the World Health Organization
(WHO), both located in Geneva, and the International Bank for Reconstruction
and Development (IBRD), located in Washington, D.C.

Subregional Inter-Governmental Organizations

Scientific and technical co-operation is a major integral part of the co-operation activities of the Council for Mutual Economic Assistance (CMEA). A strong
scientific technological potential has been created; an extensive network of
research and design organizations has been set up; an experimental basis with
up-to-date equipment has been built; skilled scientific personnel has been
trained to tackle complex problems of modern science. The CMEA member countries
have pooled their efforts further to develop scientific and technical co-operation by holding regular mutual consultations on basic problems concerning scientific and technical policy; elaboration of scientific and technical forecasts
to cover a ten to fifteen year period and joint planning of research by interested countries in certain major scientific and technological problems; co-
operation and co-ordination in scientific and technical research; extensive
exchange of scientific and technological achievements and advance know-how;
extension of co-operation in the field of scientific and technological information, invention and patents; expansion of co-operation in training scientific
personnel; organization of co-operation in the field of materials and technical

supplies which involves deliveries of equipment,instruments and material of
scientific and technological research. The CMEA secretariat is located in
Moscow. The work in the building field is co-ordinated by the CMEA Standing
Commission on Construction which meets twice a year and has a large number of
subsidiary working parties and groups of experts. The work is highly decentralized with one of the member countries taking the lead for each specific
project. In the last few years, the activities of the Commission have concentrated on new technologies for the construction of building and civil engineering works, improvement of the quality of design solutions, reduction of
time limits required for the design and construction of buildings, expansion
of the volume of production, improvement of the quality of building materials
and problems of mechanization. During 1976–1980, work is expected to be initiated on the development of methods of testing and assessing the ergonometric
parameters of building machines and the preparation of relevant normative documents.

The European Economic Community (EEC) attaches great importance to research and
development work. One of the Directorates General deals exclusively with overall
policies in this field. A special activity aimed at the co-ordination of research in the field of building materials and construction has recently been
initiated within the framework of the Directorate General of Industrial and Technological Affairs (DG III). The main objective of this initiative is to determine the means and potential of building research and development work in EEC
member countries, establish a common classification system of national research
projects, identify research fields of common interest (in particular those related to the alleviation of technical and legal obstacles to trade and harmonization of building regulations) and promote a better dissemination of knowledge on the progress accomplished in the implementation of research projects
of common interest.

The Nordic countries maintain contact in the field of building research and
development work through regular meetings of the directors of the national
building research institutes. Building research policies are also dealt with,
as required, in the context of co-operation among Nordic countries in the Nordic
Committee on Building Regulations (NKB) and the Nordic Council of Ministers
(NCM).

Non-Governmental International Organizations

A large number of non-governmental international organizations have a direct
or indirect interest in building research and development work (see annex I).*
Some of these organizations are mainly concerned with the promotion of research
and the utilization of research results. Other organizations are actively engaged in research, studies and development work, while again others are mainly
interested in the dissemination of information and documentation. The professional organizations are often active in the three fields but also take a
specific interest in research and development work as an important area of work
for their members.

As far as the non-governmental organizations are concerned, it appears that
international collaboration in the field of building research and development
is at present concentrating on problems of architectural and engineering design

---

*A concise description of each of the most important organizations is pro-
vided in Annex II, p. 82.

and, to a lesser extent, on problems relating to the production and use of building materials and components and construction technology and economy. Much less attention is being paid to problems related to the modernization, maintenance, management and use of existing buildings (see table 1).

When reviewing the activities of the international organizations concerned with building research and development, especially from the ECE point of view, it is also important to have an idea of the membership structure of the different organizations. A tentative analysis of the various organizations in this respect is presented in table 2. As will be noted, some organizations which are mandated to work on the world level, draw their main membership from European countries. Also, some "European" organizations, especially the associations of manufacturers, actually include members primarily from western Europe (ECCS, EURIMA, IECS, UEATC). Other "European" organizations actually extend their membership outside Europe (CEB, EAEE). Generally speaking, the professional organizations and some of the most specialized organizations have the widest coverage in terms of participating countries (FID, FIB, IABSE, IASS, ISSMSE, RILEM, UIA, and WFEO).

Co-ordination of International Activities in Building Research and Development Work

As pointed out in the CIB report, the activities of that organization are strongly decentralized. The main work is carried out in a series of working commissions and steering groups, varying widely in scope, nature and methods of work (e.g. "Tolerances" (W49), "Industrial buildings" (S66), "Building economics" (W55), "Housing sociology"(W69)). The initiative to set up a new CIB Working Commission or Steering Group is generally taken by one or several members of CIB. The Programme Committee, a subsidiary body of the CIB Board, is responsible for reviewing ongoing activities and examining proposals for new working commissions and steering groups. The responsibility for developing the work in each Working Commission resides with its co-ordinator, assisted by one of the members of the Programme Committees, serving in the capacity as adviser. The functioning of the Programme Committee is therefore primarily one of progress checking and co-ordination.

As to the activities of the other non-governmental organizations, the co-ordination and co-operation machinery is fragmentary or non-existent. However, under the provisions of its "co-ordination mandate" the CIB has initiated informal collaboration arrangements with RILEM (materials testing), with CEB, ECCS, FIP, LABSE and RILEM (structural safety) and with CEB, ECCS, FIP, IASS, IABSE, RILEM (building and civil engineering). The latter collaboration (the "Liaison Committee") is primarily aimed at an exchange of information on research programmes and the establishment of a co-ordinated list of meetings. Co-operative links have also been established between the CIB and the CIE (lighting and illumination research).

As noted above, the Working Party on the Building Industry of the ECE Committee on Housing, Building and Planning performs a co-ordinating function with regard to research activities related to regulations for buildings and building machinery. A first step was taken in June 1975, when the Working Party

TABLE 1 Activities of International Organizations Concerned with
Building Research and Development Work

	Principal Interest		
	Promotion of research; utilization of research results	Research, studies and development work	Dissemination of research results; documentation services
A. Building materials or components (Raw materials, production technology, economy, natural resources and environmental considerations)	UNCHBP UNIDO UNEP FAO ECE CMEA CEC ISO	CIB CEB ECCS EOQC FIP RILEM UEATC IUFRO NORD-TEST	CIB CEMBUREAU EUROPREFAB EURIMA EFPTM TBE UEATC ECWI UICB FID FESYP
B. Architectural design (Architecture, health, safety or comfort, user's preferences, economy, natural resources or environmental considerations)	UNCHBP UNEP WHO ECE CMEA CEC CIGR CIE ISO	CIB CTIF CIE ISB	CIB UIA CIGR FID UICB CIE
C. Engineering design (Structural safety and loads, economy, durability, natural resources considerations)	UNEP WMO ECE CMEA CEC ISO	CIB CEB CTIF EAEE ECCS FIP IABSE RILEM IASS	CIB FID UICB
D. Construction (Technology, economy, productivity, organization, management, environmental considerations)	UNCHBP UNIDO UNEP IBRD ECE CMEA ILO ISO	CIB CEB ECCS FIP	CIB FID UICB IECF

TABLE 1 (cont'd)

	Principal Interest		
	Promotion of research; utilization of research results	Research, studies and development work	Dissemination of research results; documentation services
E. Modernization and maintenance (Technology, economy, productivity, organization, public participation, energy conservation)	ECE FIABCI	FIABCI UIA CIB	CIB FIABCI FID UICB
F. Operation and use (Economy organization, public participation, energy conservation)	ECE FIABCI	FIABCI CIB	FIABCI FID UICB

adopted several recommendations for CIB work (HBP/WP2/6, annex III). Later on, in March 1976, the ECE secretariat organized the first inter-secretariat meeting on the harmonization of the technical content of building regulations, to which all organizations concerned with research and standardization activities related to building regulations were invited. Further inter-secretariat meetings are planned to be held both on general and specialized topics. A co-ordinating effect is also expected to be achieved through the regular sessions of the Working Party and its specialized ad hoc meetings, to which all interested non-governmental organizations are invited. Such specialized meetings were held in 1977 on regulations concerning structural safety and loads (Vyskov, Czechoslovakia, 9-13 May 1977) and on fire regulations (Budapest, Hungary, 14-18 November 1977). In addition, a meeting on programmes and priorities for international standards works and approvals in the building field (covering also pre-standardization activities) was held in Geneva from 9-23 December 1977.

Apart from the above-mentioned initiatives, which are mainly based on persuasion and mutual benefit, it is obvious that those organizations responsible for the allocation of funds for research and studies in the field of building and civil engineering (especially UNEP, IBRD, EEC) could contribute significantly to more deliberate efforts towards systematic programming and co-ordination.

Dissemination of Information on Research Programmes and Research Results, Documentation Services

From the point of view of governments, a principal means of achieving economies in building research and development work is to ensure a systematic exchange of research programmes and a wide dissemination of research results. In view of the large amount of relevant documentation available in this field, it seems vitally important to policy-makers to have available the required information presented in a concise and easily accessible form. As reported by the CIB

TABLE 2   Membership of International Non-Governmental Organizations Concerned with Building Research and Development Work

ORGANISATION	Membership				
	CMEA[a] Countries	EEC[b] Countries	Other ECE[c] Countries	Non-ECE Countries	Total
CEB	7	8	11	7	33
CEI–Bois					
CEMBUREAU					
CIB	7	8	12	24	51
CIE					30
CIGR					
CTIPEF					30
EAEE	6	4	8	8	26
ECCS	0	6	8	1	15
EFPTM					
EOQC	7	7	7	0	21
EURIMA	0	6	2	0	8
EUROPREFAB	2	6	7	0	15
FEANI	1	9	8	0	18
FESYP					
FIABCI	0				35
FID	7	8	12	35	62
FIEC					
FIG	4	9	11	17	41
FIP					72
IABSE	7	8	13	40	68
IASS					60
IECF	0	9	8	0	17
ISB					
ISSMFE	5	8	12	23	50
IUFRO	7	6	8	14	35
RILEM					59
TBE					
UEATC (full members)	0	6	2	0	8
UIA	7	9	15	46	80
UICB	4	6	9	4	23
WFEO	7	8	12	46	73

a/ The following ECE countries are full members of CMEA: Bulgaria, Byelo-russian SSR, Czechoslovakia, German Democratic Republic, Hungary, Poland, Romania, Ukrainian SSR, and USSR (total 9 countries).

b/ The following ECE countries are full members of EEC: Belgium, Denmark, Germany, Federal Republic of, France, Ireland, Italy, Luxembourg, Netherlands, and United Kingdom (total 9 countries).

c/ Other ECE countries are: Albania, Austria, Canada, Cyprus, Iceland, Finland, Greece, Liechtenstein, Malta, Norway, Portugal, Sweden, Switzerland, Turkey, United States, and Yugoslavia (total 16 countries).

efforts have been made in this direction. However, it seems as if no functioning system yet exists for the exchange of information on building research programmes and research results, covering all the organizations concerned. Also,
as underlined by the CIB, there is scope for improvement in the mechanism initiated by thàt organization.

Judging from the experience of the ECE in systematically exchanging information
on work programmes, an effective method consists in the preparation of synoptic
tables, illustrating the interrelationship between the research programmes of
different organizations or, within an organization, between different member
institutes. The principal idea behind the synoptic table is that it does not
impose an agreed format for the presentation of the programmes of the different
organizations or institutes. Instead, the interrelationships between different
programmes are analysed in two directions, each table illustrating the interrelationship between a specific programme and all the other programmes (see
model below).

Model of Synoptic Table *

Programme A (e.g. BRE/UK)	Programme B (e.g. NBI/ Norway)	Programme C (e.g. CSTB France)	Programme D (e.g. VUVA Czechoslovakia)	Programme E (e.g. NBRC Canada)	etc.
Project 1: (building materials)	Project 7.1 " 11.6 " 14.2	Project 2.1 " 15.6	—	Project A.37 " E.14 " 6.2	
Project 2: (building economics)	Project 6	Project 1.6 " 8	—	—	
Project 3: (design loads)	—	Project 3 " 4.6	Project A(g) " C(h)	Projects B.6 B.7, B.8	
Project 4: (housing sociology)	—	—	Projects B(a) (b) and (d) Project F	Project F.8	

etc.

Whatever method is applied for the compilation and analysis of research programmes, a minimum central effort is required to ensure a uniform approach in
the analysis, based on a full understanding of the method applied. A central
effort is also required to focus attention on possibilities of co-operation, to
make concrete proposals for action and to follow up their implementation.

Resources Available for International Collaboration

The above review of existing arrangement for international collaboration in the
field of building research and development indicates that most of the relevant
aspects are covered, although unevenly, by the CIB and a variety of other international organizations. In fact, the number of conferences, symposia, and other
types of international meetings in the field of building materials and construc-

---

*All project titles and numbers in this table are fictitious.

D

tion is so large as to make it extremely difficult to keep abreast of all the activities (the number of relevant meetings a year is likely to be in the range of 100). Though difficult to estimate, the cost of organizing all these meetings and the cost of participation and documentation must be very high. In contrast, the resources centrally available with the secretariats of the international organizations responsible for convening the meetings are extremely limited. Even the most important organization, CIB, disposes of a very small central secretariat only, which cannot be expected to do much more than handle the day-to-day business. The situation is even worse with regard to the secretariat resources available to most of the other international organizations concerned with building research and development work. In many cases, the secretariat consist of no more than a part-time official located in the offices of a national association. Though recognizing the strength of decentralization and the active involvement of members in the carrying out of international collaboration, it is clearly not in the interest of member institutes or governments that the national input and the international secretariat resources are too much out of balance. As pointed out above, certain functions of co-ordination and information exchange can be effectively discharged only if sufficient resources are available at the central point. The reinforcement of central secretariat resources should not amount to the establishment of central scientific research units, but merely ensure adequate technical and managerial backstopping and co-ordination. If this function is neglected, the efficiency of international collaboration is seriously hampered.

In the light of the above, it is recommended that countries, member institutes and other bodies participating in international collaboration on building research and development work consider increasing their support of the central secretariats of relevant organizations, in particular the CIB. If the CIB central secretariat could be reinforced, an indirect beneficial effect would accrue with regard to the activities of the other organizations since the CIB could then assume, in a more effective manner, its mandate as co-ordinator and disseminator of information in the whole field of building research and development work. One way of increasing the resources of the CIB secretariat could be to encourage more active participation of the building materials and construction industries in the activities of the CIB. Such a measure would seem all the more justified since a very large portion of all research and development work in this field is carried out within industrial enterprises and specialized branch institutes.

Points for Discussion

The following points are suggested for discussion at the seminar:

To what extent has international collaboration so far helped to achieve economy and efficiency in national research and development efforts ? (Concrete examples might be presented.)

What advantages and benefits other than efficiency and economy can be obtained through international collaboration on building research and development work ?

To what extent are all relevant aspects of building materials production and use, construction, modernization, management and use of buildings satisfactorily covered by research and development activities on the national and international levels ?

Is the present set-up of international organizations and the distribution
of work among them adequate and rational from the points of view of governments, the building materials and construction industries and other clients,
such as the users of buildings ?

What measures could be taken to achieve a more systematic programming and
a more co-ordinated implementation of international research activities
in the field of building materials and construction ? (In particular, how
could CIB's role in these respects be reinforced ?)

What could be done, in particular through the CIB, to improve the exchange
of information on research programmes and research results ?

How could the central secretariat function of existing organizations, in
particular the CIB, be reinforced ?

ANNEX I   KEY TO ABBREVIATIONS

Key abbreviation	UN a/	IGO b/	NGO c/	Title
CEB			X	Euro-International Committee for Concrete
CEI-Bois			X	European Confederation of Woodworking Industries
CEMBUREAU			X	European Cement Association
CIB			X	International Council for Building Research, Studies and Documentation
CIE			X	International Commission on Illumination
CIGR			X	International Commission of Architectural Engineering
CTIPEF			X	International Technical Committee for the Prevention and Extinction of Fire
CMEA		X		Council for Mutual Economic Assistance
EAEE			X	European Association for Earthquake Engineering
ECCS			X	European Convention for Constructional Steelwork
EEC		X		European Economic Community
EOQC			X	European Organization for Quality Control
EURIMA			X	European Insulation Manufacturers Association
EUROPREFAB			X	European Organization for the Promotion of Prefabrication and other Industrialized Building Methods
FAO	X			Food and Agriculture Organization of the United Nations
FEANI			X	European Federation of National Engineers Associations
FESYP			X	European Federation of Associations of Particle board manufacturers
FIABCI			X	International Real Estate Federation
FID			X	International Federation for Documentation
FIG			X	International Federation of Surveyors
FIP			X	International Organization for the Development of Concrete, Prestressing and related Materials and Techniques
IABSE			X	International Association for Bridge and Structural Engineering

ANNEX I (cont'd)

Key abbreviation	UN a/	IGO b/	NGO c/	Title
IBRD	X			International Bank for Reconstruction and Development
IECF			X	International European Construction Federation
ILO		X		International Labour Office
ISB			X	International Society for Biometeorology
ISO			X	International Organization for Standardization
ISSMFE			X	International Society for Soil Mechanics and Foundation Engineering
IUFRO			X	International Union of Forestry Research Organizations
JCSS			X	Joint Committee on Structural Safety (CIB/W.9)
NCM		X		The Nordic Council of Ministers
NKB		X		Nordic Committee on Building Regulations
OECD		X		Organization for Economic Co-operation and Development
RILEM			X	International Union of Testing and Research Laboratories for Materials and Structures
TBE			X	European Federation of Brick and Tiles Manufacturers
UEATC			X	European Union of Agrément Technique in Construction
UIA			X	International Union of Architects
UICB			X	International Union of Building Centres
UNDRO	X			Office of the United Nations Disaster Relief Co-ordinator
UNEP	X			United Nations Environment Programme
UNIDO	X			United Nations Industrial Development Organization
WFEO			X	World Federation of Engineers' Organisations
WHO		X		World Health Organization
WMO			X	World Meteorological Organization

a/United Nations Specialized Agency or similar United Nations organization.
b/Inter-governmental organization, not belonging to the United Nations system.
c/Non-governmental international organization.

ANNEX II

ACTIVITIES OF NON-GOVERNMENTAL INTERNATIONAL ORGANIZATIONS CONCERNED WITH BUILDING RESEARCH AND DEVELOPMENT WORK

CEB - EURO-INTERNATIONAL COMMITTEE FOR CONCRETE

CEB was created in 1953 and has presently a membership mainly drawn from Western Europe. The initial scope of CEB included the international co-ordination of research activities and the concerted study of the problems of the various structural applications of concrete with a view to obtaining a deeper understanding of the properties of materials and their composite behaviour, achieving a better functional performance of concrete structures and improving their competitiveness and economy. CEB synthesizes existing scientific knowledge, studies basic concepts, including the elaboration of a new basis and new data for the safety of structures, and formulates practical methods for the calculation and optimization of structures. The work also includes research on the unification of the basic concepts of different civil engineering works, in particular the harmonization of those relating to concrete and steel. Based on its research, the CEB prepares draft unified codes of practice for the planning, design and construction of concrete structures together with advice on their practical application to different structural uses of concrete. CEB also serves as the "lead organization" in the inter-association work on a "code of code" on safety and security of structures which is being prepared by the Joint Committee on Structural Safety (CEB, CIB, ECCS, FIP and RILEM).

CEI-BOIS - EUROPEAN CONFEDERATION OF WOODWORKING INDUSTRIES

CEI-Bois brings together the different branches of the mechanical woodworking industries and promotes research activities, through the Technical Committee and its three Working Groups in conditioning, preservation and finishing of wood; in behaviour of wood and its by-products in fire; and in techniques of fabrication and materials. CEI-Bois maintains regular relations with FAO, UNIDO, UNCTAD, ISO, ECE, CEN and other international organizations on interrelated aspects of the research work. It organizes a congress **every** year and regular meetings on the vital problems of woodworking industries.

CEMBUREAU is a trade organization of cement producers. It assists national members and specialized institutes in promoting and carrying out research but is particularly active in the dissemination of information of research results and the collection and compilation of statistics in its field of competence.

CIE - INTERNATIONAL COMMISSION ON ILLUMINATION

CIE draws its membership from 40 countries of which 30 are full members having a national Committee and 10 are observers. The objectives of CIE include the promotion by all appropriate means of the study of the art and science of lighting, the interchange of information on lighting among member countries and the preparation and publication of international agreements in the field of lighting. The work of CIE is carried out by 26 technical committees each of which is assigned to a member country. The reports and guides developed by these committees are generally accepted throughout the world.

82

CIGR – INTERNATIONAL COMMISSION ON AGRICULTURAL ENGINEERING

CIGR was set up in 1930 as a confederation of national associations of agriculture engineers, technicians and architects. The objectives of CIGR include the promotion of the art, science and techniques of agricultural engineering, the encouragement and the co-ordination of scientific and technical research in this field and the provision of documentation and publication services. CIGR has five technical sections of which section 2 is responsible for "agricultural buildings, structures and related equipment". Section 2 has established working groups on "animal housing: cattle", "basic requirements for ventilation and heat insulation" and "fittings for pig houses".

CTIPEF – COMITE TECHNIQUE INTERNATIONAL DE PREVENTION ET D'EXTINCTION DU FEU

CTIPEF was formed in 1901 as an association of national committees. At present, some 30 countries from Europe, Africa, Asia and Latin America are members. CTIPEF organizes a congress every four years which is prepared for by an international study commission appointed by the Permanent Council. Studies are carried out inter alia on methods for the assessment of fire hazards due to the use of polymers and plastic materials in building construction, calculation methods for fire resistance for reinforced structures.

EAEE – EUROPEAN ASSOCIATION FOR EARTHQUAKE ENGINEERING

EAEE is composed of representatives of national committees from European and neighbouring countries (North Africa, Middle East) interested in the subject of earthquake engineering. EAEE organizes regularly symposia and seminars and has also several Working Groups which are carrying out research and studies in the field of earthquake engineering.

ECCS – EUROPEAN CONVENTION FOR CONSTRUCTIONAL STEELWORK

ECCS draws its membership mainly from Western Europe. It concentrates on the preparation and publication of specifications for steel construction.

EOQC – EUROPEAN ORGANIZATION FOR QUALITY CONTROL

EOQC was set up in 1956 by the European Productivity Agency. At present the following 20 countries are full members: Belgium; Bulgaria; Czechoslovakia; Denmark; Finland; France; German Democratic Republic; Germany, Federal Republic of; Hungary; Italy; Netherlands; Poland; Portugal; Romania; Sweden; Switzerland; United Kingdom; USSR; and Yugoslavia. EOQC is organized in sections and committees. A section for the building sector was set up in 1976. The following Committees are presently functioning: "Education and training; Technical specification in quality and research clauses; Role of standardization in quality control; Glossary; Reliability; Sampling procedures; Producer-consumer relations. Some co-ordination is achieved with other parts of the world by participation in EOQC sections and committee meetings of experts from the American Society for Quality Control (ASQC) and the Japanese Union of Scientists and Engineers (JUSE).

FEANI – EUROPEAN FEDERATION OF NATIONAL ENGINEERS' ASSOCIATIONS

FEANI groups the National Societies of Engineers of 18 countries, mainly from Western Europe. It was founded in 1951 to study and resolve European problems which were of concern to engineers. FEANI has close co-operation with the

Council of Europe, the Organization of Economic Co-operation and Development
(OECD), the European Economic Community (EEC), the International Labour Office
(ILO), etc. FEANI is particularly interested in problems relating to the education and training of engineers and the facilitation of international exchange
of engineers and students. It also organizes international meetings and consultations between engineers, a congress every three years and seminars during each
of the two years between congresses. The main FEANI international events having
taken place in 1976 are the following: FEANI/UNESCO seminar on "Engineering and
education for environment" (Sweden) and SEFI/FEANI Congress on "Continuing engineering education" (Aachen).

FIABCI - INTERNATIONAL REAL ESTATE FEDERATION

FIABCI was founded in 1951 and has a membership drawn from Europe, Africa, the
Americas, Asia and Australasia. FIABCI has several professional sections and
permanent working committees which carry out research and studies in the field
of real estate. FIABCI also organizes regularly congresses and publishes its
documentation, such as bulletins, technical articles, Lexicon of Building Terms,
Real Estate Vocabulary, etc.

FID - INTERNATIONAL FEDERATION FOR DOCUMENTATION

FID was set up in 1895 as the "Institut International de Bibliographie". At
present, 68 countries from different parts of the world are members. The number
of Affiliates is 350: 18 international organizations, 178 institutional and
154 individual affiliates. The activities embrace co-operation with international organizations, research, terminology, linguistics, documentation, education and training etc. The work of the FID is carried out by more than ten
committees. The Committee on Research on the Theoretical Basis of Information
(FID/RI) is continuing projects for forecasting the development of science and
technical information and for evaluating world flows of documentary information.
The committees organize regularly conferences. The reports and publications
developed by these committees are generally accepted throughout the world.

FIG - INTERNATIONAL FEDERATION OF SURVEYORS

FIG was established in 1878 to bring together the leading national associations
to exchange views on matters of general interest to the profession, encourage,
subsidize and disseminate the results of professional research and discoveries
useful to surveyors in the scientific, technical, legal, economic and social
spheres, etc. The study programme of the FIG working group GA includes the
methods and accuracies for setting out and checking illustrated descriptions
for different measuring methods, methods and rules for quality control in measuring, recommendations for measuring tolerances, terminology, etc. FIG members
are often national delegates at meetings of ISO/TC59/SC4 - "Limits and fits in
building" and CIB/W49 "Tolerances".

FIP - INTERNATIONAL ORGANIZATION FOR THE DEVELOPMENT OF CONCRETE, PRE-STRESSING AND RELATED MATERIALS AND TECHNIQUES

FIP was set up in 1952 to encourage the formation of national groups in all
countries, which would be especially interested in the use and applications of
prestressing, and to exchange news and information on this relatively new process. At present, some 40 countries from Europe, Asia, Africa and the Americas
are members. The activities embrace exchange of opinions on scientific and
technical problems of prestressing, in particular by the organization of inter-

national Congresses and Symposia, the promotion of research, development work
and investigations, the publication of FIP Congress and Symposia Proceedings,
technical papers and other publications, and by the exchange of literature
between member groups. The Member Groups usually consist of a national engineering society, institute or body specifically set up to deal with prestressing.
The most important part of the technical work of FIP is that of the technical
commissions in the field of concrete, fire resistance, etc. FIP co-operates
with CEB, in particular in the preparation of the CEB/FIP Recommendations for
the design and construction of concrete structures and subsequent modifications.

IABSE – INTERNATIONAL ASSOCIATION FOR BRIDGE AND STRUCTURAL ENGINEERING

IABSE was established in 1929 to deal with all problems of planning, design
and construction in the field of structural engineering. Presently its membership embraces 50 countries. The objectives of the IABSE include the promotion
of international collaboration between engineers and researchers, the exchange
of technical and scientific knowledge, the publication of experience and results
of research and the organization of scientific meetings, symposia and congresses.
The work of IABSE is carried out by national groups, which organize their own
meetings and issue their own publications and by the Technical Committee which
co-ordinates the technical activities of five working commissions and two working groups in the following fields of activities: concrete, steel, metal and
timber structures, contractors and constructions, structures and system analysis, etc. The IABSE publications are published annually in two editions which
contain reports of the working commissions, congress reports on studies, experiments or results of research, and the bulletins also containing special scientific or technical articles.

IASS – INTERNATIONAL ASSOCIATION FOR SHELL STRUCTURES

IASS was set up in 1952 with the purpose of organizing meetings and congresses
for the interchange of ideas in the field of reinforced concrete shells, reinforced ceramics, wood, plastics, etc., when these form a continuous surface,
as well as when a plane structure consists of triangulation or cables, such as
hanging shells. IASS activities include the dissemination of periodical publications, the creation of working groups to investigate and report on special
topics of the relevant technology, and the collaboration with other similar
organizations.

IECF – INTERNATIONAL EUROPEAN CONSTRUCTION FEDERATION

IECF is an organization interested in the development of regulations and standardization in construction. The technical development of the construction
industry is of direct concern in this field of work. The IECF has created a
permanent technical commission responsible for reaching the goals through research work, seminars, exchange of experts, etc. The pursuit of the goals is
also carried out by the member countries of IECF through delegates of national
organizations of contractors participating in technical research and standardization work.

ISB – INTERNATIONAL SOCIETY OF BIOMETEOROLOGY

ISB was founded in 1956. A few years ago it started to pay attention to the
building field. Thus, for example, ISB co-operated with the CIB, the WMO and
the IFHP in organizing the Symposium on "Climate and Living Comfort", held in
Zürich in 1974.

ISO – INTERNATIONAL ORGANIZATION FOR STANDARDIZATION

ISO has a total of 81 members, of which 33 are from the ECE region. It is a non-governmental organization, although 70 per cent of its members are governmental agencies or public bodies. Being the principal organization responsible for international standardization activities, ISO is one of the main users of research results of other international organizations and also one of the main producers of material of interest to intergovernmental bodies. Consequently, ISO co-operates with a large number of other organizations, both intergovernmental and non-governmental. Close links have been established between the ISO and the ECE, particularly in connexion with the ECE programme on the harmonization of the technical content of building regulations. The preparation of ISO International Standards is highly decentralized. It is almost exclusively undertaken by Technical Committees, Sub-committees and Working Groups, which are serviced by individual national standardization bodies. ISO activity in the field of building has developed rapidly during recent years. In order to achieve a better overall programming and co-ordination of standardization activities in this field, a Technical Division on Building was established in 1972. In 1976, this Division set up a small Divisional Council, inter alia, to ensure continuous co-ordination in between Technical Division meetings.

ISSMFE – INTERNATIONAL SOCIETY FOR SOIL MECHANICS AND FOUNDATION ENGINEERING

ISSMFE membership is made up of National Societies within six regions – Africa, Asia, Australasia, Europe, North America and South America. Each of the National Societies regularly arranges symposia and conferences every four years. The proceedings of these various symposia and conferences provide a valuable source of reference for engineers and scientists in soil mechanics and foundation engineering. The Society has a number of Sub-Committees such as Standardization of Penetration Testing in Europe, Exchange of Geomechanical Computer Programmes, etc.

IUFRO – INTERNATIONAL UNION OF FORESTRY RESEARCH ORGANIZATIONS

IUFRO was founded in 1956. Its research work is carried out by 41 Subject Groups and 18 Project Groups in the following 6 Divisions: Site and Silviculture, Forest Plants and Forest Protection, Forest Operation and Techniques, Planning, Economics, Growth and Yield; Management and Policy; Forest Products, General Subjects. The research work in IUFRO is expanding not only into new fields – such as environmental management and education – but also geographically. Results of IUFRO's work are disseminated in the form of special articles, the publication of the proceedings of seminars, symposia, etc. These publications are distributed to all member institutes.

RILEM – INTERNATIONAL UNION OF TESTING AND RESEARCH LABORATORIES FOR MATERIALS AND STRUCTURES

RILEM was founded in 1947 as an organization for directors of laboratories. It is the policy of RILEM to deal only with testing methods and, in this connexion, it has close co-operation with ISO. RILEM recommendations are published chiefly concerning the testing of concrete. However, RILEM's twenty technical committees cover the testing of timber, durability of concrete, light-weight concretes, non-destructive testing, synthetic resins, concrete admixtures, corrosion of reinforcement, bituminous materials, and many other specific aspects of material testing. The activities of technical committees often start and/or end with a symposium. About 50 symposia have already been organised by RILEM.

UEATC - EUROPEAN UNION OF AGREMENT TECHNIQUES IN CONSTRUCTION

UEATC is an association of national organizations responsible for assessing and sometimes certifying new products and innovations in building. At present the following eight countries are full members: Belgium; France; Germany, Federal Republic of; Italy; the Netherlands; Portugal; Spain and the United Kingdom. UEATC issues Common Directives by which products tested for approval on a national basis might be accepted without recourse to further assessment or testing for use in similar situations in other member countries. The Agrément is created for the benefit of its users (architects, designers, builders, etc.) to give a complete technical information service about a precise definition of products' composition and method of manufacture, performance characteristics under specific conditions of use.

UIA - INTERNATIONAL UNION OF ARCHITECTS

UIA draws its membership from eighty countries in five geographical regions. Every three years an Assembly takes place, as well as a World Congress open to all those interested. In the interim, many different meetings are held mainly at the regional level, organized by the Commissions on "Professional Practice" and "Architects Education", as well as by the Working Groups: "Town Planning", "Housing", "Construction and Industrialization", etc. They undertake studies and research of general interest or specially requested by international organizations, such as UNESCO. Each year the UIA organizes or helps to organize international competitions in architecture and town planning.

UICB - INTERNATIONAL UNION OF BUILDING CENTRES

UICB was formed in 1959 and now has 36 members in 22 countries of the world. It is a forum for the exchange of information, technical documentation and discussion on all questions which affect the running of a Building Centre. The Directors of member centres of the UICB meet regularly every three years in order to hold their General Assembly. The UICB has set up working groups to discuss and study selected problems in the field of building. UICB collaborates with the international organizations on all questions concerning architecture, town planning and building and fosters professional exchanges by means of congresses, exhibitions, international competitions, study tours, meetings, books, bulletins, etc.

WFEO - WORLD FEDERATION OF ENGINEERS ORGANIZATIONS

WFEO draws its membership from 72 countries of Europe, Africa, Asia and the Americas. The objectives of the Federation are to advance engineering as a profession in the interest of all people, to encourage the application of technical progress to economic and social advancement throughout the world. WFEO fosters engineering education and training, encourages the exchange of engineering information and sponsors scientific and engineering meetings, symposia and congresses, etc.

OTHER NON-GOVERNMENTAL INTERNATIONAL ORGANIZATIONS CONCERNED WITH
BUILDING RESEARCH AND DEVELOPMENT WORK

Apart from the above listed organizations, the following have an interest in
or actively promote building research and development work:

- Battelle Institute
- Bouwcentrum International Education Foundation (BIE)
- European Ceramics Association (AEC)
- European Development Fund (EDF)
- Fédération Européenne des Fabricants de Tuyaux en Grès (FEUGRES)
- European Federation of Fibreboard Manufacturers
- European Federation of Manufacturers of Refractory Products (PRE)
- European Federation of the Plywood Industry
- European Federation of Pottery Tile Manufacturers (CEC)
- Fédération Européenne des Fabricants de Tuiles et de Briques (TBE)
- European Federation of Parquet Manufacturers Unions
- European Federation of Particle Board Manufacturers (FESYP)
- European Federation of Sanitaryware Manufacturers (FECS)
- European Federation of Unions of Joinery Manufacturers
- European Information Committee for Lightweight Facades (CEIFAL)
- European Organization for the Promotion of Prefabrication and other Indus-
  trialized Building Methods (EUROPREFAB)
- European Union for the Scientific Study of Glass
- International Association for Asphalt used in Construction
- International Association for Hydraulics Research (IAHR)
- International Association for Waterproofing
- International Bureau of Precast Concrete
- International Federation of Building and Woodworkers (IFBWW)
- International Federation of Christian Trade Unions of Building and Wood
  Workers
- International Federation of Consulting Engineers
- International Federation for Housing and Planning (IFHP)
- International Heating and Air Conditioning Federation
- International Institute for Land Reclamation and Improvement
- International Institute of Welding (IIW)
- International Road Federation (IRF)
- International Union of Associations of Heating, Ventilating and Air Condi-
  tioning Contractors
- International Union of Building Societies and Savings Associations
- International Union of Local Authorities (IULA)
- International Union for Roofing, Plumbing, Sanitary Installations, Gas and
  Water
- Trade Unions International of Workers in the Building, Wood and Building
  Materials Industries
- Union of National Federations of Negotiators in Construction Materials in
  the EEC

APPENDIX

RESPONSE PAPERS

GOALS AND PRIORITIES

Finland

THE ORIENTATION OF BUILDING RESEARCH IN THE PUBLIC SECTOR

The framework for the planning of building research can be described by the following distribution:

- 65 per cent of the building research is financed by the private sector,
- 20 per cent by the public sector,
- 15 per cent by others, such as professional organizations, foundations, etc.

The public sector is responsible for 90 per cent of basic research and 60 per cent of applied research. Trade and industry finances 90 per cent of the developmental work and 25 per cent of the applied research. The work done by the professional organizations and foundations, etc., covers about 80 per cent of standardization and 15 per cent of applied research.

Links between the Societal Objectives and Research Policies

The organization of public research in Finland can be described mainly as bipolar. On the one hand, there is the general research system supervised by the Ministry of Education, to which all universities and institutions for higher education have been subordinated. This system is especially responsible for basic research. On the other hand, the task of the other ministries is the guidance and administration of the applied research and development needed in their branch of administration.

These two systems are coordinated at a higher level by the Science Policy Council, the task of which is to help the Government and its ministries in the handling of important issues concerning the improvement of scientific research and research training. The chairman of this Council is the Prime Minister. Other members are six Ministers and some experts on scientific research. This Council has published a programme for national science policies, which is the overall research policy programme in Finland. It has been asserted in this programme that scientific research must be in harmony with the developmental goals democratically set by society.

The Science Policy Council hardly touches private research in its programme, though it considers that a great responsibility for realizing the programme lies with the private sector. A separate committee composed of representatives of industry, government and the trade union movement has been set up for this purpose. Its task is to study the possibilities of increasing the research pursued by private enterprise and of directing it so as to achieve the goals of industrial policy and general science policy in our country.

Goalsetting in Building Research

In addition to these societal objectives for research set by the Science Policy
Council, there has not been any overall programme for building research and
development. Different bodies have financed and programmed quite independently
the research and developmental work in their fields.

The National Housing Board, subordinated to the Ministry of the Interior, works
out research programmes to contribute to the realization of goals in the governmental housing policy. The Ministry of Trade and Industry, its appropriations
for the promotion of technical research pursued by industry, and the Technical
Research Centre subordinated to the Ministry, have an important position in
research co-operation between government and industry. The Academy of Finland
(central body for science administration subordinated to the Ministry of Education) is responsible for the basic research needed in building.

Because of dispersion in the building sector problems have emerged concerning
the coordination of building research. Due to this situation there have also
been weaknesses in mutual information about research results. To improve the
situation, the Delegation of Planning and Building Research has been set up
by the Ministry of the Interior, which is in charge of controlling and directing physical planning, and building seen from the point of view of the public
interest, as in safety and health questions.

The Delegation consists of representatives of Ministries (the Ministry of the
Interior, the Ministry of Agriculture and Forestry, the Ministry of Trade and
Industry, the Ministry for Public Transport), Government Central Offices (Nat-
ional Housing Board, National Board of Agriculture, National Building Board,
National Board of Public Roads and Waterways, Academy of Finland), universities,
units representing intermediate and planning, and the Technical Research Centre.

The main tasks of the Delegation are the orientation and coordination of building and planning research according to the developmental goals of society and
according to the needs manifested in decision-making and in the improvement of
the planning and building system. The promotion of the utilization of research
results is an essential part in its work. The Delegation is the body which trans-
forms the research objectives set by the Science Policy Council in the field of
building and planning into a concrete research programme, which could serve as
a basis for financing the research. The elaboration of this programme is now
going on in the Delegation.

An important feature in the working out of the programme is the intersectoral
approach to problems in the building field. Also the composition of the Delegation (representatives from both building and planning sectors) present excellent possibilities to analyse building problems from new points of view by
examining, for example, the interaction of the planning and building processes
and its connections with the quality of the built environment.

In activating the programming of research and developmental work according to
administrative needs and to those of promoting building production, there is
the danger that the ministries and industry assume a too-dominating influence
on research as a whole. Research oriented mainly by practicians tends to become too short term in its nature. The best way to avoid this disadvantage is
not to let them have too much impact on the research supplied via the general
research system supervised by the Ministry of Education. This research should
be independent, critical, and at least partly basic in its nature.

Kirsti Vepsä:
the National Housing Board of Finland

The authority in Finland responsible for housing administration is the National Housing Board, which is subordinated to the Ministry of the Interior. The functions of the National Housing Board include the handling of state loans for housing production and the implementation of government measures aimed at the development of housing production and improvement of housing standards.

The National Housing Board is responsible for the preparation of an overall research programme in which the different fields of research and research plans are listed in their order of implementation. This general programme is revised annually by the Council of Housing in the Ministry of Interior and is subject to approval by the government.

The Objectives of Housing Research

In formulating the objectives of housing research and in deciding the lines along which research is to proceed, the basic aims both of scientific and research policy and of housing policy have to be taken into account.

Under the Housing Production Act, housing research funds may be appropriated for the purposes of social, administrative, economic and technical research on housing production, experimental building activity, the use of housing, other areas of housing policy and the translation and publication of the results of such research or the translation of foreign material into Finnish.

The goals and means of housing policy, production and building of dwellings and houses, quality standards and building and running costs are defined in the National Housing Programme which also directs housing research.

The Areas Studied

In the 1970s, some two-thirds of the appropriations were used for technical and economic research and one-third for social and administrative research. The main emphasis in housing research activity is currently changing from research concerned with reducing the investment costs of housing production and increasing the efficiency of building by co-ordinating dimensional systems, to a greater concern with reducing the running costs of existing buildings and of housing areas and with the properties of buildings in use. Greater emphasis is also placed now on research into ways in which the requirements set by the needs of the public, different forms of housing, ways of life and the desire to increase housing security can be taken into account in planning and implementing building designs and the organization of financing, building and production.

Research Needs of the Near Future

Housing research should not take into account only those problems which are
currently in the foreground in housing policy and in the design and implementation of dwellings and the housing environment. It should also bear in mind
the rise in the demand level which accompanies the process of social change;
it should aim at forecasting these changes and at developing new approaches to
housing problems. In the sector of house construction the main problems are

- building cost and running costs of the existing housing stock,

- energy costs associated with new housing production and renovation,

- the system of use, care and maintenance of the existing housing stock.

Application of Research Results

Housing research financed by the Housing Board has a certain advantage in that
the same organization both defines the goals and supervises the research activity and makes the decisions. In spite of this, there are some difficulties
involved in applying the research results effectively.

The Housing Board has tried to solve the problem as follows. Every research
project is supervised by a group comprising the users of the research concerned
in the Housing Board, in different ministries and in central planning and building organizations.

The Housing Board started three years ago the project "conditions for low-rise
house building" in order to make the planning and building of houses rational
both for the national economy and the private household. In the supervisory
group are representatives of technical, economic and social research, planning
and building, including the producers of materials and components.

The advantage of this course of action is that the users of the research can
already during the research process express their own views on setting the
objectives and - which is important - on how the research results are presented
in order to minimize the so-called "application gap".

In addition to the above-mentioned way of utilizing the research results the
Housing Board makes a condition in the research contract that research results
should be disseminated in newspapers, journals and publications.

The German Democratic Republic

I. DEFINITION OF SCOPE FOR BUILDING RESEARCH

Objects of Building Research

In previous discussions it has already been pointed out that an essential difference between "building science" and other sciences is to be seen in the fact
that building science cannot be confined to a single research object to be attained by a single scientific discipline. Research objects in building are characterized by multiplicity and complexity, which frequently necessitate the participation of various disciplines of fundamental and applied research, thus involving scientific disciplines other than building research as well.

Objects and scope of building research in the German Democratic Republic are
defined in accordance with the social and economic targets set by the Government and the internal economic and technical reproduction process of building.
These goals are at present defined as follows:

— to provide sufficient and high-quality housing for every citizen including
  the social and communal facilities in a pleasing urban environment;

— to further develop and rationalize industry and energy supply as a basis
  for national economy;

— to raise the technological and economic level of building production and
  ascertain high quality and optimal reliability of building products;

— to make fuller use of domestic raw materials and secondary raw materials
  and to apply material-saving and energy-saving structures;

— to rationalize preproduction processes of technical preparation and the
  design process in particular;

— to improve working conditions for building workers and workers employed in
  the building materials industry and in prefabrication.

The scope of building research in the German Democratic Republic is established
within the framework of the international scientific and technological cooperation among the countries of the CMEA. The main line of the scientific-technological policy in building in our country is to further develop industrialization
of building with due regard to the application of economic lightweight construction.

The field of scientific and technological objectives dealt with by building
research in the GDR is very broad indeed. It may be subdivided into the following groups of problems:

Building Products and Techniques:

- building materials (chemical and physical properties, manufacturing processes);

- building structures (properties of structural mechanics and physics, optimal design);

- finishing processes and heating, ventilation and sanitary engineering;

- building design (appropriate functional solutions for residential and civic buildings, for industrial and agricultural buildings, etc.);

- special-purpose structures (for industry, power industry, water supply, transport and environmental planning);

- prefabrication;

- site operation (new building and rehabilitation by industrial methods, techniques of underground engineering);

- construction equipment (further development and effective utilization of machinery and equipment for prefabrication and site operations);

- processes of transport, handling and storage in building;

- design processes, standardization and economic planning processes.

Cross-Sectional Fields (Interdisciplinary Fields):

- theoretical engineering concepts (structural mechanics, soil mechanics, structural physics, architectural acoustics, protection against corrosion, fire protection, etc., and building regulations);

- fundamentals of construction techniques (reliability of technical systems, measuring and testing techniques; automation);

- application of cybernetics and automation to construction techniques, to design processes and economic planning processes;

- ergonomics and occupational medicine;

- economic fundamentals of the internal technical and economic reproduction process in building;

- town planning and environmental planning (including sociological investigation);

- history and theory of architecture;

- planning and steering of scientific work and technical information in building.

Scientific Disciplines Involved in Building Research

Natural Sciences. Fundamental research in mathematics, physics, chemistry, etc., is not conducted within the framework of building research. But results of research undertaken in these fields are systematically being made use of. In the first place, this applies to the fields of building materials research, structural calculation, applied mathematics, cybernetics and computer technique, the relation between man and his environment in respect to regional planning and socialist town planning.

Technical sciences such as material science, structural mechanics, the theory of reinforced concrete, structural physics, architectural acoustics, research on corrosion, thermodynamics and fluid mechanics in HVS-equipment, aerodynamics of structures, etc., are considered to be constituent parts of building research. Various other fields such as reliability of technical systems, automation and electronic data processing may also be included in building research to some extent. The Academy of Building, institutes of technology and universities are particularly concerned with the subjects mentioned above.

Economic Sciences. Research on economics of building in the German Democratic Republic is largely concerned with the improvement of the centralized national planning methods for the building sector and with industrial engineering.

Research on construction systems as to their economic parameters is of specific importance in view of the large investments provided for by the building industry. Both development and design of structures and construction systems in their close relation to building design and techniques are to be analysed under various economic aspects.

Jointly with building research institutions in the USSR, research is being carried out on the development of probabilistic-economic calculation methods for building design.

Social Sciences. Studies in the field of social sciences and sociological research pertaining to the relation of man to his living and working environment are being conducted within the framework of building research, jointly with the research institutions of the Academy of Sciences and the universities and colleges.

Human Sciences (Medicine). Results obtained in the field of human sciences are made use of by research for residential and civic building, industrial building and town planning. Of particular interest is the study on the effects of the micro-climate on man, the results of which are taken into consideration in building hygiene.

In the building sector of the GDR, there has been established a special scientific-technical centre for ergonomics to study questions of occupational hazards (labour safety) and industrial medicine.

Applied Mathematics. More recently particular interest has been focused on the application of mathematics to all branches of building research in the German Democratic Republic. The efforts are aimed at a rational employment of mathematicians to increase efficiency of research work.

Applied mathematicians employed in building research are expected to develop suitable mathematical models for technical, economic and organizational problems given and they are to prepare algorithms to solutions and aid their computer-based implementation. Close co-operation between mathematicians and specialists of the respective disciplines is an important prerequisite to finding optimal solutions.

Types of Building Research

The group of problems listed on page 90 embraces subjects of fundamental research (on natural sciences, technology, economics, social sciences), of applied research and development as well as specific forms of technology transfer
(industrial scale application).

The overwhelming majority of the building research potential, concentrated in
the Academy of Building and the building industry, is directed, within the
framework of the sixteen current research projects, towards the preparation
and working out of solutions to development and rationalization of products
(building materials, building components, complete buildings and structures of
all kinds), of technologies (raw materials industry, prefabrication, site operations, underground engineering operations, transport processes) and rationalization of design processes and town planning.

Of the total potential of the building research, 15 - 20 per cent are employed
to create a scientific reserve and to prepare studies on theoretical fundamentals in selected fields of research. In the German Democratic Republic there
has been prepared a draft catalogue of fields of research for the building
sector.

In accordance with the science policy defined by the government there have
been developed, in some fields of building research, specific branch-oriented
potentials of fundamental research. These potentials have the objective to
transfer, via building research, into "building practice" the results of fundamental research conducted by the Academy of Sciences, universities and colleges. Conversely, the tasks of building research have to be introduced into
technical and natural science fundamental research.

An effective collaboration is being developed between teams of branch-oriented
fundamental research in building and the respective institutes of the Academy
of Sciences.

II. CHOICE OF RESEARCH OBJECTIVES AND DEFINITION OF PRIORITIES

The distinction of research objectives and research problems made by Mr. Bertière
in his introductory report applies to building research in the GDR as well.
These objectives have been defined as follows:

- general objectives established by the Government;

- specific objectives, forming part of the general objectives, and being a
  subject of building research;

- clearly defined objectives which are assigned to each research programme
  subject.

Research problems have been divided into:

- basic problems of national importance and subject to government supervision;

- ministerial problems, considered to be important at the ministerial level;

- problems of specific importance to particular branches, and subject to supervision by the respective enterprise or association of enterprises.

According to the second paragraph of this paper, the assignment of the overall economic, political and social objectives at the governmental level is
given in the National Science and Technology Plan, drawn up by the Government
of the GDR. The Centralized Science and Technology Plan, prepared by the Ministry of Building, encompasses, apart from the objectives of the National Plan
for the building industry, tasks and groups of problems relevant to the Ministry
of Building.

Subjects relevant to individual branches are covered by the Science and Technology Plans of the associations of enterprises and individual enterprises,
respectively. The plans of enterprises include those tasks of National or Centralized plans, for which the enterprise concerned is responsible.

The basic principle underlying planning on the three levels mentioned is to
ascertain a unified scientific-technological policy. This is achieved by the
National Plan in the framework of the Government, by the Centralized Plan of
the Ministry of Building in the framework of the building sector of the country, by the Science and Technology Plans of the enterprises in the framework
of the different branches of the building sector and the individual construction firms.

Research subjects are defined in the following way: For the main development
line of GDR's building a systematic forecasting is prepared covering the period of the next following 15 - 20 years. This forecasting effort will mainly
be carried out by institutes of the Academy of Building in collaboration with
the most important research institutions of the building industry. Forecasting
data will then offer a basis on which the elaboration of branch-oriented concepts for the building sector will be prepared, for a period of, say, 10 - 15
years. For the same period, the research concepts for the building sector will
be drawn up by the Ministry of Building, in conjunction with the Academy of
Building.

A more detailed elaboration of research subjects will then be prepared in the
form of scientific concepts for the individual research areas (for a period of
10 - 15 years) and by programmes for separate research projects (covering a
period of 5 years).

Research programmes and scientific concepts form the basis for medium-term
planning (5 years) and annual planning as well. The research subjects of the
current science and technology plan (covering a period of one year) will be
further split up for the individual research teams and listed in so-called
"assignment folders".

The choice of research subjects and establishment of priorities will be object-
ified by presenting forecasts, building research concepts as well as research
programmes and scientific concepts to examination through specialists working
groups appointed by the Ministry of Building.

Further identification of plan tasks is achieved by pre-established general
objectives of governmental interest, set up by the Ministry or other decision-
making bodies. The general objectives will then be assigned to the respective
research establishment, which works out the draft plan to be, in turn, examined and approved by the decision-making body. Working groups of specialists

and consultants will again take part in the process.

Finally, the assignment of tasks for new research projects and the plan tasks completed will be investigated and approved by working groups of specialists. In this investigation process, important suggestions will be made for an efficient implementation of the respective subjects and their subsequent transfer into technological practice.

Pertinent choice of research tasks and definition of priorities have proved to be essentially dependent on the selection and qualification of the representatives sitting on the working groups. Following that experience, the establishment of a system of specialized working groups is intensified by the Academy of Building, within the framework of sections of its plenum. Representatives of building research, experts from the construction industry and design profession, professors in civil engineering and scientists of various other disciplines sit on these working groups.

Criteria for the choice of research subjects are determined, on the one hand, by the yield of measurable economic effects (in terms of reduced costs and man hours, savings in materials and energy) and, on the other hand, by general benefits to the community, not quantifiable in economic terms, such as improvement of living and working conditions, higher quality of urban planning and conservation of the natural environment, etc.

For each research subject to be included in the Science and Technology Plan, the planning authorities call for a detailed description of economic effects and general benefits to the community as well as for the implementation of subjects via large-scale application of research results.

In order to avoid the risk of concentrating research efforts solely on short-term profitable subjects with the ultimate neglection of the necessary reserve capacities, the following steps are being taken:

Building research potentials are directed towards two basic objectives:

  - the yield of new scientific-technological results of international standard;

  - the rapid transfer of results to industrial production and application in other community spheres.

Key factors for the transfer of scientific and technological results are seen in the fields of design and technology. Building research and technology in the German Democratic Republic are directed towards working out generalized solutions in order, if need be, to avoid seeking additional solutions to each new problem arising.

As has been suggested, apart from carrying out high-priority tasks in building research, aimed at objectives of specific importance to the national economy and the community in general, certain discipline-oriented areas of research are being developed with the aim to provide the necessary scientific foundations for applied building research, to close the gap between pure research, conducted by institutes of Academy of Sciences, on the one hand, and building research on the other hand, and finally to create a basis for a stable long-term development of building research potentials.

In the German Democratic Republic the view is held that fundamental research on building is not just to serve the creation of a more or less vaguely defined reserve capacity. Instead, it should yield, from the outset, real effects, be it materials or energy savings, reduced costs, increased labour productivity, improved working and living conditions or conservation of the natural environment.

Current work is being concentrated on the problems of practical application of results of pure research to building design, technology and the design process. Transfer of results is to be achieved via the preparation of respective documents, regulations, rules, test programmes and computer programmes, tailored to user requirements.

The Federal Republic of Germany

Building is a comprehensive task whose impacts cannot be delimited. The research tasks to be performed both for the theory and the practice of building are just as comprehensive. The goals of this research are: a liveable built environment, buildings which meet human needs and allow people to freely develop their personality, improved quality and productivity including the resultant positive effects on cost trends, and improvements in the production process which are last but not least in the interest of those employed in this process.

In the Federal Republic of Germany building research tasks are performed in the following way:

- the building materials and construction industries carry out applied research and development;

- federations and associations concentrate their efforts on those fields of applied research which correspond with their functions. An example of such a research institution is the internationally well-known German Committee on Reinforced Concrete;

- foundations normally provide funds for basic research;

- research assistance by public agencies or individuals or bodies receiving public support is granted both for applied and basic research. For development assistance — which is particularly expensive in the building sector as well — only very few public funds are allocated.

Because of the scarcity of funds earmarked for research assistance and of the insufficient research capacity — which is in turn a result of, among other things, these narrow means — priorities must be set:

- in the industry, it is the market which sets the priorities;

- federations and associations engage in only such activities as correspond with their members' interests;

- foundations either concentrate their efforts on predetermined purposes or they work on the basis of programmes set up and adjusted by their bodies;

- for publicly supported sponsors and public authorities, e.g. the Federal Ministry for Regional Planning, Building and Urban Development, the promotion of building research is a general as well as a specific departmental task. Priorities are determined on the basis of practical needs and pre-set political targets. Public sponsors will also try to find and eliminate gaps left by research so far. With research assistance coming from so many different sources, some overlaps inevitably occur which require

103

special attention. The same applies to certain fields of an interdisciplinary nature for which neither of the many agencies promoting research
is willing to assume sole responsibility.

As an example, the way shall be described in which research priorities are determined in the Federal Ministry for Regional Planning, Building and Urban Development. When determining research priorities, use is made of the Working
Group on Building Research (Arbeitsgemeinschaft für Bauforschung (AGB)) in
which almost all institutions concerned with building research promotion in the
Federal Republic of Germany are grouped together under the chairmanship of the
Federal Minister for Regional Planning, Building and Urban Development. An
iterative procedure is used to determine priorities for research assistance on
an empirical basis. A research programme exists which is adjusted annually.
The whole complex of research activities is subdivided into thirty-four fields
of study. It is from these fields that proposals for adjusting the research
programme are made, based on the experience gathered in the annual discussions
of the research proposals submitted. The proposals are compiled and submitted
for re-examination to the experts working in the above-mentioned fields of
study; these are invited to pay particular attention to the fact that their
own priority proposals should be in a reasonable proportion to those submitted
by their colleagues from other fields. The results are then submitted to the
AGB's Research Council who gives its opinion on them and may make its own proposals. It is on the basis of the AGB's list of priorities that the Federal
Minister for Regional Planning, Building and Urban Development determines the
priorities of his own research programme. All researchers are then informed
of the co-ordinated programme by circular letter from the Federal Ministry.
Applications for research assistance by the Federal Minister which can be
easily incorporated into the framework set by the research programme will have
a good chance of success. Part of the funds available, however, is reserved
for work which cannot be included in the programme, for example work initiated
to meet a departmental short-term need. Thus, new promising proposals are giv-
en a chance even if they cannot be incorporated into the overall research programme.

The 1977 Research Programme includes the following elements:

focal point: housing needs, quality of housing, behaviour of residents,

- improvement of the use value of dwellings in particular by a more practical technical equipment,

- housing needs, behaviour of residents;

focal point: modernization of old buildings,

- organizational ways and means of improvement, e.g.

  - co-operation,

  - co-ordination,

- technical questions, e.g.:

  - improvement of thermal and sound insulation,

  - modernization of service and technical equipments,

  - use of new building materials and construction methods;

focal point: planning in housing construction,

- improvement of modular co-ordination,

- development of preferred dimensions, in particular for storey and room heights, building components and elements as well as interior works; type standardization,

- development of tolerance systems and corresponding measuring and control systems,

- measurability and assessability of planning activities,

- cost-benefit analyses;

focal point: stabilization of building activities,

- possibilities of and prerequisites for stabilizing building demand and production,

- possible ways and means of stabilization by medium-term financial planning on the local government level,

- possibilities and limitations of the use of planning leads (i.e. of keeping a reserve of orders),

- improved transparency of the building demand,

- relation between the structure of company sizes and stabilization,

- questions relating to a continual working to capacity of building companies applying industrial production methods;

focal point: rationalization and industrialization of building,

- more functional building elements and components,

- possible compatibilities,

- optimum employment of operating funds,

- forms of co-operation (vertical and horizontal),

- standardization of functional invitations to tender and spatial programmes in housing construction; development of a practicable operational concept,

- possibilities of serialization,

- co-ordination of the planning, preparation and financing of construction and actual construction processes,

- possibilities of limiting construction costs,

- questions relating to industrial production,

- methods of connecting; joints;

focal point: constructional physics,

- suitability of building materials, in particular of new building materials and structures, and their performance with respect to constructional physics,

- methods of testing from the point of view of constructional physics, in particular with a view to their employment on site,

- thermal insulation, energy savings,

- sound insulation against exterior noise,

- sound insulation for dwellings with light-weight outer walls and flexible ground plans;

focal point: new building materials and new building technologies,

- stability and continuous performance of new building materials,

- studies on economic efficiency,

- possible ways of and areas for application in housing,

- combination of various materials; compatibilities,

- development of uniform testing and control methods;

focal point: interior work and service and technical equipments in housing,

- improvement of the use value of dwellings by a more practical technical equipment,

- rationalization and industrialization of interior work and service and technical equipments,

- co-ordination of interior work and service and technical equipments,

- interchangeability of elements; type standardization; development of preferred dimensions;

focal point: information

Projects by which the flow of information and the application of research findings can be improved are a particular concern to the Federal Minister for Regional Planning, Building and Urban Development.

- preparation of crosscut and summary reports on "the state of the art" in individual fields of study or important subsections;

- evaluation and processing of research findings from individual fields of study and translation of those findings into a form suitable for practical application;

- gathering of new findings from abroad;

- concerted information on rationalization methods.

The promotion of building research activities in the Federal Republic of Germany is still insufficient. According to present investigations — which are, however, not absolutely reliable — only about 1 per cent of the funds turned over in the building industry is spent on building research. All in all, these funds which are raised by industry, associations and federations, foundations, public authorities and individuals or institutions receiving public support amount to DM 140 m. On the average, DM 60,000 are spent on each research project receiving assistance from the Federal Minister for Regional Planning, Building and Urban Development. What is urgently needed is a more comprehensive concept of building research. However, it would seem of little use to develop such a concept without making sure in advance that the funds required for its application are available. Proposals to this end have been submitted, based on ideas and experience from other European countries.

As long as the funds earmarked for building research have not been significantly increased, building research will have to concentrate on a few goals and priorities. Due to the situation in the building sector, primarily those research activities must be supported which will have a stabilizing effect on construction costs without necessarily causing a reduction in quality.

Hungary

TECHNOLOGICAL FORECAST OF THE HUNGARIAN
BUILDING INDUSTRY UP TO 2000

Forecasting of the technical development of the Hungarian building industry
started from the recognition that scientifically well-established long-term
plans have to be based on forecasts of informative character which, explor-
ing and analysing the laws of motion of development, investigate the expected
fulfilment of these laws over a period exceeding the term of the actual plan
period.

The revolutionary trends in contemporary science and technology have a many-
sided impact on the building industry. On the one hand, with the expansion of
these trends higher requirements are imposed on the building industry and on
the other, building industrial development and its material conditions undergo
substantial transformation.

The most important trends taken into account in establishing the principles of
long-term technical development are described below.

The general trend of the urbanization process is of basic importance. The main
building industrial development trends directly related to urbanization are the
following:

— rising trend of the vertical dimensions of buildings;

— growing tasks in construction below grade, with the increase of quantitative
  and qualitative requirements for public utility and other installations below
  grade;

— growing number and quality of building services equipment;

— increase of the economical size and equipment level of community
  establishments;

— creation of the conditions for estate-type housing construction.

In the development of the Hungarian socialist building industry it was building
industrialization that brought about the most revolutionary qualitative change,
a consequence comprehensively derived from the natural development trend according to which an increasing portion of building processes are transferred
from building sites to highly mechanized permanent plants.

Further factors influencing the technical progress in the building industry
include

— the analysis of foreign building industrial development;

— the expected trend of the international division of labour;

— the development of the professional structure of the building sector;

— the development of communication and transport facilities;

— expected variation of the technical standard of other sectors of production;

— further increase in the difference between the physical and moral obsolescence periods;

— expected changes in the standard of living, conditions of life, production
  technologies, use of leisure time, social, cultural and health provisions,
  etc.

The careful, many-sided weighing and analysis of all these factors provides a
realistic basis for specifying the long-term principles and aims of the technical development of the building industry.

During the coming 20-25 years a development at a rate higher than the average
can be expected in the chemical and plastics industry, the exploitation of el-
ectric power, agricultural production technologies, food processing and can-
ning industries. Nuclear engineering industry and the extension of the peace-
ful uses of atomic energy affecting various sectors can be expected to undergo
rapid development and to raise peculiar requirements in respect of the building
industry.

The rising standard of education, training, health protection will have considerable impacts on the technical development of the building industry. The
growing amount of leisure time, the changes in the style of living all have
an impact on its future tasks.

Environment protection activities in progress all over the world will certainly
have many building industrial consequences.

Taking all this into account the main trends of the development to the Hungarian building industry and the basic direction of its technical improvement
in the period up to 2000 can be forecast as follows:

— Up to 2000 the production of the socialist building industry is expected to
  increase 3.0-3.5 times as compared to the present figure assuming no change
  in prices.

— Production expected in transport construction, municipal and foundations
  engineering and urban construction below grade will increase at a rate highly
  exceeding the average of building industrial production.

— An increase in the proportion of maintenance construction is expected in the
  first half of the period only.

— During the coming 25 years a significant increase in the number of building
  industrial employees cannot be expected. In the other branches of industry
  an increase is, however, expected in the amount of live labour engaged in
  the production of products ultimately used by the building industry (materials, structures, appliances, equipment).

— A considerable change can be expected in the average skills and professional
  structure of workers and employees in the building industry and in the proportion of workers employed in plants of permanent location. Main characteristics of the change: doubling of the present proportion of engineers and
  technicians, including the trebling of the proportion of mechanical engineers,
  decrease by half of the proportion of unskilled workers, trebling of the
  proportion of steel structures fitters, welders, machine operators and mech-
  anicians; decrease of the ratio of bricklayers, navvies, transport workers
  and loaders.

— The basic trend of technical progress in the building industry for the next
  quarter of the century remains industrialization, in progress since 1960.

— In the period to come, one of the fundamental ways of the further development of industrialization is to develop the network of plants of permanent
  location and to improve the joints and system components of various building
  systems in a unified modular system, the combinative application of system
  components based on which system building is promoted further. The importance of the application of system building lies mainly in that it facilitates
  the increase of the size of production series to an extent greater than ever.

— In projecting plans of buildings, in selecting the materials and structures
  and in dynamic and thermal dimensioning the endeavour becomes stronger and
  stronger to use as little energy as possible during the erection and lifetime
  operation of buildings.

— The spatial dimensions of buildings will increase considerably. In housing
  construction the average number of stories will increase from the present
  2.7-3.3. to 3.8-4.5 stories. The average number of dwellings
  per building will approximately double. The average size of industrial
  buildings expressed in cubic metres will double or triple and that of
  communal buildings will increase between 150 and 200 per cent.

— Profound changes are to be expected in the technologies of building construction. The main characteristics of these are the following: modular dimensioning, structural joints of the various construction methods, construction technologies will approach each other and facilitate the combined application of
  interchangeable system components.

— In civil engineering a considerable increase in the average dimensions of
  construction projects can be expected. This retroacts on the technological
  development and mechanization of construction. The average performance of
  civil engineering machinery will increase at a rate exceeding that of the
  total building industrial machinery.

— The volume and proportion of underground construction increases.

— The rearrangement of the structural composition of materials and structures
  used in construction and with it the decrease of the weight of the building
  per unit area will continue. The weight per $1 m^2$ of area of the building can
  be expected to decrease from the present 1.6-1.7 tons to 1.1-1.2 tons in housing
  construction, from 1.3-1.4 tons to 0.7-0.8 tons in communal construction, substantially improving the conditions of the transport background inherent in
  construction.

— Of the materials used in construction the proportion of steel, aluminium,
  plastics, glass and various insulating materials will increase. On the other
  hand, the specific application of the various brick types, cement, heavy concrete without reinforcement, stone and sand will decrease.

— The number and total performance expressed in horse power of machinery in the
  building industry will continue to increase. Machine performance per worker
  will presumably reach 12-15 h.p. in the state-owned building industry and
  10-12 h.p. in socialist building industrial co-operatives.

— The proportion of building services engineering will increase. This is an

E

inevitable consequence of the increased water and power requirements of the use of buildings, of the improved standard of modern conveniences.

— The overwhelming majority of the technological processes of interior works will be realized during the course of structural construction.

— A serious improvement of the organization level and a substantial decrease in the duration of construction work can be expected.

— In the two-and-a-half decades to come international technical-scientific and economic co-operation will take a strong upswing. This applies especially to the purchase of building machinery, to trade in the field of system components, to building design and scientific research as will as to licence and know-how exchange.

— In addition to the above the technical development of the building industry has to serve the constant improvement of the technical culture and working conditions of building industrial workers. Great emphasis must be laid on the re-education and extension training of workers in accordance with the professional requirements raised by new building methods.

Hungary

In Hungary, building research/development work is undertaken on a contract basis. All design/construction/investment organizations have the right to have their technical problems solved, innovation tasks worked out by professionally competent research institutes, refunding the costs incurred by the latter. Similarly, the various authorities (Ministries, supervisory Boards) secure the results of research/development activities they deem necessary by issuing contracts. These are essentially contracts for "work, labour and material" suitable to financially sustain the research institutes concerned. A disadvantage, occurring especially in the field of company contracts, is that such contracts are generally issued on a short-term basis, are oriented towards solving the problems of a particular restricted field and lack the comprehensive development works and underlying research available in the broader fields.

The authorities supervising building research in Hungary (in particular the Ministry of Building and Urban Development) therefore organize priority programmes to realize the comprehensive central goals which have an impact on the building sector as a whole. Priority programmes having life-spans of 5-10 years aim at definite goals and results, including the subordinate tasks to be solved. During the course of research work attempts are made not only to describe the results but also to specify a system of conditions for adaptation providing an appropriate basis for the decision process of the leading authorities of the building sector. Priority programmes are managed by Programme Committees, including as members, in addition to leading officials of the building sector, scientists, researchers, heads of university chairs of the given profession and experts of the construction industry.

Priority programmes are financed from the central development funds of the Ministry. To attain the goal in an efficient way the Priority Programme Committee is in charge of establishing an interrelated system of research-development projects and of controlling their fulfilment, being under obligation to report yearly on the progress of work.

As regards their weight two types of priority programmes can be distinguished in Hungarian practice:

- government level high priority nationwide programmes (concerning several sectors) and

- sectoral priority programmes (particularly concerning one sector of the national economy).

The priority programmes having an impact on the building sector are at present:

GOVERNMENT-LEVEL HIGH-PRIORITY PROGRAMMES

Central Research into Industrialized Lightweight and Mixed Construction Systems

The aim of the programme is to promote the domestic application of all building methods of industrialized character, suitable for considerably reducing the duration of on-site construction work, transferring the greater part of production processes to permanent prefabrication plants. These methods also applicable in other building systems, facilitate the mass and serial production of structural elements, resulting in a significant decrease in the specific expenditure requirement of building industrial work.

In its first phase, the programme aims at promoting the adaptation of the complex lightweight construction method, using steel, aluminium, plastics, wood, fibre board and glass, a method constituting one of the main features of "system building", while in its second phase it extends to all building technologies which can be developed into building systems by themselves, or in combination with each other, especially in combination with certain structural components.

Development of Environment Protection

In this field it is the aim to work out measures to reduce detrimental effects, to specify technical requirements, to work out methods of calculation, and settlement policy principles for the complex design of buildings and settlements to develop sociological, health, technical-economic appraisal procedures.

Up to 1980 research in Hungary will be concentrated on the protection of the flora and fauna in surface and underground waters, on waste disposal, on the protection of the ecological system as well as on the preparations of practical measures. Surveys on the detrimental effects of construction activities are also in progress.

SECTORAL PRIORITY PROGRAMMES

Mechanization and Automation of the Transport, Handling and Loading of Building Materials and Components

Thirty per cent of the live labour capacity is engaged in the moving of building materials in factories as well as in and between building sites. The aim of the priority programme is to decrease this percentage by one-third in the fifth 5-year-plan period.

Development of Foundations

The priority programme foresees technical-economic solutions which raise the standard of the design of foundations, and decrease live work and financial expenditure.

Development of Private Housing Construction

Technical conditions have to be created for privately owned housing to be realized by organizations and technologies much more up to date than previously. Efforts have to be concentrated on the development of grouped or estate-type housing construction.

Automation of Building Industrial and Silicate Industrial Production

The aim is to select and automate the processes of concrete production and prefabrication, concrete curing and to introduce the computerized control of technological processes.

Further Development of Large Concrete Panel Construction

The network of prefabrication plants having been completed, a further aim is to improve modular co-ordination, to bring the technological processes of prefabrication up to date, including the decrease of specific live labour expenditure. Simultaneously with the realization of planned reconstruction, the conditions have to be created for producing dwellings of larger areas in the long-term plan period, and for applying lightweight construction systems and components in prefabrication.

The programme includes the modernization of box units, the widening of their selection, the development of cladding and surface treatment procedures and panelized systems for communal buildings. In the field of technological development the problems of finishing works, containerization and automation have to be solved. In building organization work information systems are to be improved and the application of computer techniques introduced.

Development of Urban Construction below Grade

Tasks to be solved: In the plan period residential estates comprising more than 1000 flats are to be provided with tunnels integrating the various public utility ducts and pipelines. In households, particularly in hot-water supply, gas is to be replaced by some other energy carrier in about 100,000 dwellings.

Development of Energy Rationalization in the Building and Building Materials Industry

The aim is to explore the architectural means of energy conservation with a view to the energy-saving solutions of siting, orientation, architectural layout and structural development. Optimization of the hygrothermal properties of buildings, modernizing of heating systems, development of energy-saving aero-technical equipment. Development of energy-saving concrete technologies.

Development of Maintenance Construction Work

The aim is to work out norms and guiding principles for maintenance construction work and the management of buildings.

Building Research-development Projects in Connection with the Application of Nuclear Power

The aim is to improve the technology of protective concrete barriers for reactors, to define the requirements of construction, technical regulation and environment protection in connection with the location of nuclear power plants.

The Application of Computers in Building

The purpose to be attained is to develop and apply computerized methods in management at ministry and company level and in technical design.

Complex Scientific Research into Regional Planning

A registration and information system connected to the information system of the building sector is to be established for regional planning. The aim is to co-ordinate sectoral land use requirements for a better conservation of natural resources, by the use of the registration, information and regulation system.

Industrial Processing and Application of Perlite

The priority programme includes as major aims the solutions of the problems occurring in the mining, expansion of perlite, in the manufacture and use of perlite products, the development of prototype equipment and the increase of perlite exports.

Netherlands

PREAMBLE

Building research is instrumental to society's ultimate goal to shape and use
its built environment to satisfy its present and future needs at acceptable
costs.

Every subject of building research should be placed in this context, and thus
be recognized as simultaneously having relevance to one or more elements of
the inherent multi-dimensional problem field; pertinent factors may be:

Phases of the development process of building	Problem aspects	Objects of the built environment	Partners in the building process
Inventory of users needs	Functional	Countries	User
Drafting of programme of requirements	Technical	Regions	Principal
	Economical	Towns	Architect
	Conceptional	Quarters	Consultant
	Regulative	Buildings	(Sub) contractor
Design	Decisional	Houses	(Supplier)
Realization	Operational	Components	
Use		Materials	

Conclusions relevant to the restricted field of building materials, components
and construction are not necessarily valid for other areas of attention, or
even for the totality of building research.

GOALS AND PRIORITIES

Goals

Data should be obtained, and pertinent insight evolved and disseminated, with
regard to:

- factors determining user's appreciation of the built environment
  as a place for living and working;

- factors influencing the quality of built environment and that of
  individual buildings or other objects built;

- factors that improve the management and control of the built environment and promote its optimum condition;

- macro-economic and market-technical factors playing a role around the built environment;

- socio-economic, proper functioning of the building industry; with specific attention being paid to:

> management studies;
> promotion of productivity in the building process;
> promotion of opportunities for product innovation;
> labour aspects.

To be on the look-out for signals from society indicating changes in the pattern of expectations as regards built environment, in terms of needs and available means, and to implement the relevant consequences.

To feed the continuous process of changes in the built environment with technical and procedural methods, with particular emphasis on the decision-making process, and - in that respect - on the improvement of the communication process.

To maintain an R&D institution with adequate staff and facilities to execute its task.

To convert knowledge acquired through R&D into practical advice.

Priorities

In the near future, attention will particularly have to be paid to the following activities:

Integration of contributions made by social sciences within the process of decision-making.

To design and implement a system enabling quick, clear and regular reception of signals bearing on qualitative and quantitative needs for building.

To establish, as clearly as possible, sufficient characteristics of built environment in order to draw policy-conclusions from them.

To define, as clearly as possible, characteristics that make an environment attractive for living.

Promotion of methods and techniques enabling participation of non-technical parties in the decision-making process.

To evolve a systematic approach for choosing between action aiming at either new buildings or renovated buildings, with emphasis on support in solving problems emerging from practice.

Efforts towards a system of open standardization.

To study the consequences of a position, adopted consciously, over against the energy problem and scarcity of certain materials. To indicate suitable solutions.

Systematic approach for problems of maintenance, including their consequences at the design-stage.

Objective and proper formulation of safety and security requirements, also
in their mutual relation, to be satisfied by buildings and other objects
built.

Recognizing that, as regards current building methods, considerable scope
for saving of costs should be sought in finishing techniques, contributions
to related problem solving are imperative.

To pay attention to new means aiming at improved communication around
the building process.

Sweden

Building research of a more continuous and systematic nature was begun in
Sweden during the 1940s. To start with the focus of this research was both social
and technical. Social studies were aimed at describing the standard of homes
and their suitability for different types of household. Technical studies were
aimed at testing and developing new building materials and at improving the
kitchen equipment, bathroom standards and storage and washing facilities of the
individual home. Thus technical studies were also intended to adapt homes more
closely to the users' requirements. Another purpose of technical studies was
to provide documentation on which to base the industrialization of building.
This aspect of technical building research was reinforced later in the 1950s
and in the 1960s when the volume of housing production drastically expanded.

Current building research preserves this combined social and technical approach.
The aim is to develop within the building sector a technology which will meet
all the various demands made of the end product, within the framework of the
resources available. Technology must measure up to users' demands concerning
safety, security, variation and beauty, but it must also develop with proper
regard for general economics and the economics of production. In recent years
building research has also been enlisted in the service of energy conservation
to a greater extent than previously. (On this point see Olof Eriksson's response
paper on the following pages.)

Building research in Sweden is not only aimed at furnishing documentation for
the formulation of functional requirements, etc., for buildings and constructions. An important sector of building research is also concerned with process
questions, i.e. the way in which the built-up environment comes into being and
is maintained and transformed. Among other things, process research is important because possibilities must be created for the development of direct user
participation in the evolution and administration of homes, working premises
and communal amenities. Wider user influence demands not only greater research
into processes but also the communication of research findings to users on the
same self-evident terms or to public authorities, clients and the building
industry.

Research contributes in various ways towards the development of new products.
One of the important purposes of research is to obtain new knowledge. Research
creates a fund of knowledge which constitutes the foundation of technological
development. In order to be made useful, knowledge must be made generally
known - through education and information measures, for example. Another of the
important purposes of research is to contribute towards the development of new
products and working methods. Research is often an important, though seldom
a dominant part of development work. Development work often starts with the
analysis of a problem and a discussion of the way in which it is to be solved.
Research then appears as one of the means of solving the problem. Researchers
should be brought into the problem-solving processes of public authorities and
industry at the earliest possible stage. (On this point, see response paper
by Thomas Sidenbladh on page 121.)

QUANTITATIVE METHODS IN THE DETERMINATION OF BUILDING RESEARCH PRIORITIES*

The introductory report which has been presented on Goals and Priorities describes building research activities covering many different fields, but its main emphasis is on technical research into hardware in the building process as a prelude to the concrete development of new types of building, etc. Research is gradually increasing in complexity. The problem is to find other methods than those of a qualitative nature for the determination of priorities, and the selection of projects is a matter to which great care must be devoted.

But it is also worth asking to what extent quantitative methods should be aimed at when determining priorities in the variegated and expanding field of building research.

- There does not exist any continuous process from basic research via applied research and development to a new product, a new method or process, etc. It is better to speak in terms of two processes. One of these - research - is cognitively creative. The other - development - yields new implements. The interrelationship of the two processes is a complex one, and this makes it hard to discern the usefulness of research in the development phase. Thus even if quantitative methods can be evolved for the determination of development priorities, it is not certain that they will be serviceable for purposes of research - even applied research.

- Research and development are tools used in our efforts to attain definite goals. Some form of quantitative evaluation may possibly be attached to the degree to which a project brings us closer to a particular objective, but it is also the task of research to furnish documentation for new aims in society and to analyse and criticize the manner in which we approach existing goals. Research of this kind demands other, qualitative criteria.

- Research and development must yield new technology making it possible for all the various results demanded - the ultimate built-up environment - to be achieved with the resources at our disposal. But research and development must also help to describe and explain user demands, and therefore research must include socio-economic questions. It must deal with human experience of the environment and not only with the physiological influence of the environment on the human organism. The behavioural sciences have to consider perspectives of development psychology, and so on. Great difficulties are bound to arise in the quantification of priorities for this kind of research.

- Not only must technology correspond to social demands and demands of other kinds put forward by the users of the ultimate result, it must also be integrated with the ecosystem. Locally this applies to meteorological, hydrological and biological processes. Globally it refers, for example, to demands on finite energy resources. Between the local and global contexts there are other questions concerning resources, e.g. supplies of raw materials. These are factors which probably can be quantified. But they are of great complexity, and the ramifications of positive and negative effects are virtually infinite.

- Technology is more than hardware. It also includes software - the processes whereby the built-up environment comes into being, is maintained and transformed. We also speak of planning, building and administration. Research

---

* Compiled by Olof Eriksson, the Swedish Council for Building Research.

and development must focus more upon these processes as such. When this is done in a rationalization perspective, it may be possible to define quantitative priorities for research and development. But these processes also constitute the occupational environment of the persons employed in building and administration, and they must therefore be made the subject of labour science research which is completely different in nature from research aimed at rationalization and is therefore less easily managed in terms of quantitative priorities.

- There are also other sides to these processes. For example, it is obvious that the laying out of industrial facilities simultaneously with the construction of large housing areas is a rational procedure in the narrow context of business economics. But this process also entails the concentration of large numbers of people in one place within a short period. The social process whereby a collection of people develops into groups and a society with a sense of community is one that cannot be artificially accelerated. When people are denied the opportunity of participating in the planning and building process, they are also excluded from activities which could be catalysts in the creation of community sense. Sometimes this exclusion results in social problems. Often such problems are ascribed to the physical design of the building development, but it is arguable that they are no less due to the design of the building process. It is not axiomatic that industrial building can be combined with greater participation. Research and development concerning process questions have to take both aspects into account, in which case the aims of research and development cannot be expressed solely in quantitative terms.

One hazard of quantitative methods of determining priorities is that questions which can only be treated qualitatively are given a zero rating. In other words, they are edged out of the system. Now that building research is faced with broader tasks in fields where qualitative assessments of research inputs are the most reasonable approach, methods of qualitative assessment will have to be sought and developed.

THE LINK BETWEEN RESEARCH AND TECHNOLOGICAL AND ECONOMIC DEVELOPMENT*

It is almost an axiom of social debate for research to be closely related to the technological and economic development of the community. This relation is often taken to imply that basic research leads to more applied research, which in turn forms the foundation of technological development work. The final link in the chain is the production and marketing of the end product.

This view of things prompts the conclusion that, in order to promote the technological and economic development of the community, efforts must be devoted to research. In order for research findings to be disseminated and utilized, extensive information measures are organized to transmit knowledge to potential users.

This view, however, is not borne out by international studies. There have been cases of the results of technological research being put to immediate use in industrial development work, but far more often research findings have not been applied until long afterwards.

* Compiled by Thomas Sidenbladh, Ministry of Industry.

International studies present a different picture of the industrial development process. The aim of this process is to develop new products, processes and systems. Research, on the other hand, is aimed at the acquisition of new knowledge. The development process is triggered off by the awareness of a need or of certain technical possibilities. This generates an idea concerning technical solutions or concerning possible fields of application for a given technique. The realization of the idea often calls for extensive development work, and in the course of this work one often finds research as a necessary but insufficient means of obtaining successful results.

Economic anticipations are one of the motive forces of the industrial development process. The success of development work is often defined in terms of profitable sales. In this way development work differs from research, which is often prompted by quite different considerations, e.g. the desire for new knowledge or academic qualifications.

Research affects the industrial development process in many different ways. As mentioned above, one of these is the role of <u>research as an important but not always paramount part of development work.</u> Another is <u>the contribution of research to the corpus of knowledge</u> which constitutes the foundation of technological development. If knowledge is to be utilized it must be widely disseminated, which it is, for example, by its incorporation in the training and education of technologists and other occupational groups. Perhaps education is the most important route towards the utilization of research findings. Thus the third way in which research affects industrial development is when people who have been involved in research subsequently change to industrial activities, taking with them their knowledge and experience of scientific methods.

With certain modifications, the above model of the industrial development process and of its connection with research is applicable to every field in society where efforts are made to solve problems by methodical means. The first stage is for the problem to be defined and for ideas to be conceived regarding its solution. Research then comes on the scene as one of the means whereby the problem is to be solved.

The researcher should start to influence the problem-solving process at the earliest possible stage. Scientific viewpoints can then be balanced against economic and political considerations. If the researcher does not come on the scene until research work begins, his chances of exerting influence will be considerably less.

Summing up:

1. Research investment does not lead to increased industrial development work.

2. Increased support for industrial development work leads among other things to an increase in applied research.

3. In a market economy, support for industrial development work must be designed in close co-ordination with the measures taken by firms themselves, and it must above all concentrate on those stages of the process where the measures taken by firms, seen from the viewpoint of society, are either inadequate or misguided.

4. Research is a necessary and important precondition of more long-term technological development.

5. Investment in industrial development work must therefore be accompanied by investment in basic research.

The United Kingdom

How and by whom should goals and objectives of building research
be clearly defined?

How and by whom can general building research objectives be transformed
into detailed programmes and how can qualitative objectives be transformed into quantitative targets?

As the introductory discussion papers all emphasize, building research nowadays
covers a broad range of disciplines, including the physical and social sciences,
a spread of types of research extending from directed basic research to prototype development, various kinds of research organization (government, academic,
industrial, etc., with their different financial arrangements), a wide variety
of users of research results, and a complex network of information flow amongst
them. This makes it difficult to answer the above questions definitively, yet
they are at the core of the problem of utilizing resources efficiently in building as in any other applied research.

In the United Kingdom it was consideration of such questions as those which led
to the principle enunciated by Lord Rothschild in his paper "A Framework for
Government Research and Development 1971" which has been accepted as a basis
for all applied research and development (R&D) within the UK central Government.
The principle is that applied R&D, that is R&D with a practical application as
its objective, must be done on a customer/contractor basis. The customer may
be direct (the user of the product, process or method of operation which is the
outcome of the research) or indirect, in that he represents the user of the results. Thus, within the Department of the Environment, the policy administrators
are direct customers for the research which aims to provide a basis for improvement in the policies they administer. At the same time, the Department sponsors
research for the benefit of the users of buildings (the population at large)
and is in this sense an indirect or proxy customer. It is incumbent on government departments to carry out or to buy the research needed for the efficient
carrying out of their functions.

In principle the customer says what he wants and the contractor does the research. In practice the matter is not quite so simple as this, and it may be
useful to outline the organizational machinery which is being developed in the
UK on the basis of experience gained in applying the Rothschild principle over
the last 5 years.

The major block of work served by the machinery to be described constitutes
the research programme of the Department of the Environment (DOE). Some of the
programme is carried out within the Building Research Establishment, which
forms part of DOE; some within DOE Headquarters and some within organizations
under contract to or supported by the Building Research Establishment or DOE
Headquarters. The organizations which carry out this contract research work
are to be found in industry, in industrial research associations and in institutes of higher education.

The aim of the organizational procedures which have been evolved is to ensure that research proposals are based on a thorough and effective dialogue between the user and the researcher - the customer and contractor respectively in the terms used by Lord Rothschild. The dialogue takes place at various levels. At the top, broad allocations of funds are made, and guidance about the objectives of the Department is issued in general terms; at the other extreme, working-level discussions between user and researcher are carried on often informally Research proposals are evolved within the constraints set by available resources of money and expertise, and are expressed in the form of "Programme Items" which cover in the same format the following:

- an outline description of the work proposed;

- its objectives;

- the size and nature of the relevant market for the research;

- previous progress if work on the subject already in hand;

- expected progress in the first year of the work;

- means of application of the results of the work;

- resources required in terms of men and money.

The Programme Items, typically describing work costing £50,000 per annum, are the conceptual building bricks which are assembled to form the Department's overall research programme. For management purposes, a smaller unit, a more limited research project, is often involved.

Research proposals are formulated by agreement between contractor, customer, and the central research policy staff whose duty it is to make sure that adequate discussion takes place. The actual proposals are submitted by those responsible in DOE for the initiation of the work, and many come from the contractors. The feasibility, usefulness and timeliness of the work are examined jointly by representatives of customer, contractor and central research staff, who have a collective responsibility to assemble Programme Items to form coherent packages (termed for convenience "Subject Areas" representing typically £0.5 million) which compete for resources through the operation of higher-level committees.

The rules of this competition are inevitably fluid to some extent, because likely future needs for expertise (some of which inevitably arise suddenly but have to be foreseen as far as possible) have to be kept in mind. It is recognized that the essentials for successful dialogue between customer and contractor are mutual understanding of both responsibilities and the limitations within which each works. Inevitably, differences of opinion arise which have to be resolved at higher level.

An important point is that the resources for research do not "belong" to the customer. Within the Department, it is the responsibility of the Director General of Research (DGR) to ensure that customer needs are met as efficiently as possible within the constraints of the resources (which are allocated to him, not to the customers). An important instrument in discharging this responsibility is his Directorate of Research Policy (DRP) - the central research policy staff mentioned above, who have research experience but are not, in their role as mediators, generally responsible for the management of research projects.

During each year, all the research proposed for the coming year is formulated at the level of description mentioned above. The DRP co-ordinates the views expressed in the various committees and advises DGR on allocation of resources. Equally, the dialogue enables the Director of BRE and others to satisfy themselves about the scope and balance of the parts of the programme for which they are responsible and about its influence on the continuing scientific health of their organizations.

The process can be seen looking from the top as the allocation of resources in terms of finance and expertise in the light of past performance and likely future needs. Seen from the bottom, it is one of aggregating research proposals to form coherent programmes, within policy guidelines.

The major responsibility for ensuring that proposals are well thought out rests with small groups representing contractor, customer and central research staff. Since programme formulation is an art as well as a science, freedom to exercise judgement is essential, and much formal and informal consultation is involved. Advisory bodies range from the high-level Construction and Housing Research Advisory Council, which covers the whole field of building and construction research, down to working parties which discuss research formulation and application in detail, and typically cover one to three Subject Areas (research costing from about £0.1m.to £1m.per annum). The Building Research Establishment also has advisory committees at various levels through which views from outside government are also brought to bear. Although these advisory bodies are not formally part of the resource allocation machinery, their influence is not inconsiderable. It is felt nevertheless that their influence should be increased to counteract the tendency toward inward-looking which might otherwise arise when resource allocation is based on a tightly knit government research contractor - government customer dialogue.

Cost-benefit analysis would perhaps be expected to be an important tool, but it has to be said that this has found very limited application to UK building research, largely because of the complexity of the application chain, although it has been applied throughout the programme of research relating to road and bridge design and construction. The notion that likely benefits must be estimated and judged in relation to likely costs, however, is fundamental to the discussions.

The foregoing arrangements apply to research which the Department of the Environment either carries out itself or lets under contract. There is other building research, still within the public sector, where other arrangements apply. Other government departments such as the Department of Education and Science and the Department of Health and Social Security have research programmes of their own involving building. All work on the customer/contractor principle and contact is maintained between them and with the Department of the Environment through various interdepartmental committees. Universities and polytechnics also do building research, some of which is sponsored directly by DOE, as has been mentioned.

Other building research is paid for by public funds through the Science Research Council, where industry, government and the academic interests are represented on the appropriate committees. The aim here is not to generate a coherent research programme in response to specific customer needs but to stimulate good-quality research with application much in mind.

Four research associations, the Construction Industry Research and Information Association, the Timber Research and Development Association, the Building Services Research and Information Association and the Water Research Centre receive financial support from public funds through the Department of the Environment. General support is increasingly being replaced by grants for research in selected areas and by work placed under contract in conformity with the customer-contractor principle.

For completeness, mention should also be made of the building research carried out by public authorities such as nationalized industries and local authorities. Throughout there is liaison, but these bodies are, of course, responsible for their own expenditure.

It will be seen that the core of the UK building research effort lies within the Department of the Environment. The Building Research Establishment plays a leading role, carrying out itself research costing about £8.6m. per annum out of a total Departmental building research expenditure of around £11.9m. The organizational machinery to which most attention has been given in this note is therefore that of DOE, where the machinery seems to be intermediate between that of Hungary and that of France.

ORGANIZATION, STAFFING AND FINANCING

Finland

Organization

Building and planning research in Finland is carried out in the Technical Research Centre, in government agencies, in the engineering departments of the universities, as well as in the research laboratories of industry.

The Technical Research Centre (VTT) is the main government research institute in Finland with three research divisions: the Division of Building Technology and Community Development, the Division of Materials and Processing Technology and the Division of Electrical and Nuclear Technology.

VTT aims to meet the research and testing needs of public and private sectors and to maintain and raise the level of technology in Finland. The main fields of activity at VTT are research, development and testing, as well as participation in national and international collaboration, and administrative and supporting services. The R&D activity is divided into basic research (10 per cent), applied research (70 per cent) and development work (20 per cent).

The main research fields of the Division of Building Technology and Community Development are for the time being: building materials technology and recycling, energy conservation, production technology and economics, research related to general safety, community planning, municipal engineering, traffic engineering and transport economics.

The Division is divided into ten laboratories: the Concrete Laboratory, the Geotechnical Laboratory, the Laboratory of Heating and Ventilating, the Laboratory of Land Use, the Fire Technology Laboratory, the Laboratory of Building Economics, the Structural Mechanics Laboratory, the Road and Traffic Laboratory, the Building Laboratory in Otaniemi and the Building Laboratory in Oulu.

Financing and Staffing

Total running costs of the Division of Building Technology and Community Development (about 400 employees) were about 25 million Fmk (6.2 million US $) in 1976. It was covered by state budget (36 per cent), other government administration (22 per cent), industry (40 per cent), and foreign customers (2 per cent). As the share of the direct state financing is relatively small, the basic research has decreased detrimentally in some research units.

Each laboratory (on average 40 research workers) has a relatively narrow field of activity and most of the research work can be done within the laboratory concerned. Besides the linear organization a project organization is applied, especially in multidisciplinary projects. Usually these projects are financed by several sponsors.

Some Experiences

Limited research and development tasks are smoothly managed in the framework of the above-described system, especially in cases where the user of the results and the research laboratory concerned have worked in close collaboration with each other.

The fact that the financing is partly covered by the state budget and partly by commissions has in some cases activated the research climate.

The continuity of the occupation and employment of the researchers has partly been dependent on the research contracts. Attention is thereby paid to contract-based research and development.

The experiences gained at VTT showed that it is likely to find the optimum structure between the quality and profit of the research results with help of the financing policy. This financing policy has got a remarkable influence on the organization of the research work.

The main problems have been to get the projects smoothly started, to assign the responsibility to the laboratories, to disseminate the research results in practical form to the users, and to accomplish an effective research co-operation.

Information on research results is disseminated in several forms, e.g.

- publications in VTT series;

- articles in journals;

- codes of practice, instructions, recommendations, specifications, standards;

- lectures, seminars, conferences, exhibitions.

Experience shows clearly that personal contact between researcher and user is an essential channel for information. Especially in Finland where the number of users of research results is smaller than in large countries direct contact between researchers and users can be easily arranged.

Organizational structure of VTT

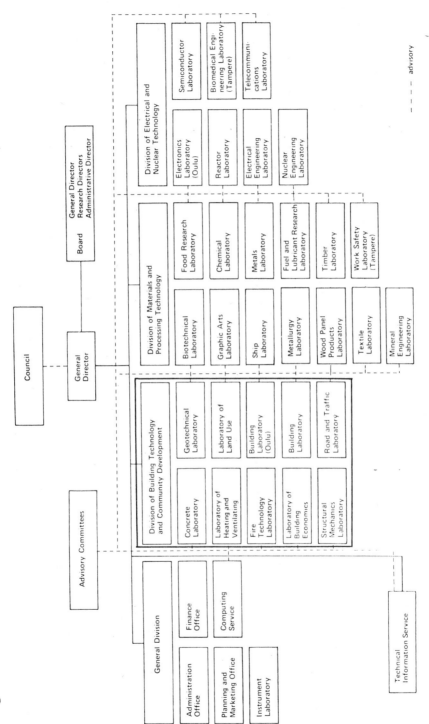

The German Democratic Republic

ORGANIZATION

In the German Democratic Republic building research and development tàsks are carried out in the following research establishments:

- in the institutes of the Academy of Building;
- in the institutes or research and development stations of the construction enterprises and combines of the construction industry and building materials industry;
- in the civil engineering colleges.

The Academy of Building as a centralized state-run research establishment is primarily concerned with providing solutions to fundamental problems of technico-scientific development in the building sector as a whole, while, on the other hand, the enterprise-based research and development stations are as a rule oriented to the immediate rationalization of production processes and the solution of specific building design tasks. To co-ordinate similar research efforts, undertaken by different enterprises, some branch-oriented co-operational units have been formed.

The Academy of Building is directly subordinate to the Ministry of Building. Its wide-ranging research efforts include the following tasks:

- fundamentals and solutions to the increased utilization of domestic and secondary raw materials such as the development of rationalized methods of production of building units or components of gypsum and anhydrite using clays and fine sands;

- research on theoretical engineering concepts (structural mechanics, soil mechanics, fire protection, corrosion protection, structural physics) to create a scientific reserve capacity for ensuring reliability of structures as well as achieving economic use of materials and energy in the construction industry;

- tasks aimed at rationalizing and developing structural design and construction methods applied in residential and industrial building, for social facilities and agricultural buildings;

- rationalization and further development of the prefabrication basis for the construction industry, primarily structures for residential and industrial building;

- elaboration of scientific prerequisites for further mechanization of site operations;

- further development of principles of urban planning and architecture as an important prerequisite for the implementation of the long-term housing

131

programme. Basic approaches to an intensified redevelopment of obsolete
buildings in city centres;

- economic fundamentals of construction, industrial engineering fundamentals
  and economy of capital funds.

In the institutes of the Academy of Building work is done on fundamental research
problems as well as on tasks of applied research and development. Efforts are
also being made to complete fundamental research findings to the extent of
being suitable for transfer to practice and made available by means of regulations, standards and other design aids.

Building research in the German Democratic Republic is primarily organized on
the basis of centralized research projects which are assigned to the institutes
of the Academy of Building or to the centrally run industry. To organize research
efforts in these institutes there have been set up special steering groups headed
by the director of the respective institute or by one of his deputies. The
steering groups work in close partnership with co-operational bodies in the
industry as well as in colleges and universities.

At present, sixteen research projects are dealt with by research in the building
sector. These research projects may be revised in their structure or new subjects added as new problems arise or if changes are necessitated from an organizational point of view.

Research projects are organized and monitored on the basis of research programmes, i.e. the formulation of research tasks as to their content, development
of research potentials as well as allocation of funds are done within the framework of the research programmes. The programmes will be drawn up for a period
of 5 years and will usually be updated annually. The research programmes include
the establishments and scientific disciplines necessary for providing the solutions to tasks, no matter of what orientation or subordination the establishments may be.

Long-term development of research potentials is achieved in the research fields,
i.e. within the framework of stable groups of problems of the building sector,
which are clearly defined in their content. The planned development of the
research field is to ensure the availability of the necessary research potential
at the time a new research project is due to be started.

The fields of research in building are primarily structured and dealt with by
the Academy of Building jointly with the colleges of technology and universities. The scientific concepts worked out for a period of 10 to 15 years are a
vehicle for management and organization of the research areas.

The Ministry of Building is the client for the major building research topics.
Branch-oriented research is commissioned by the management of the construction
industry and building materials combines.

At fixed periods or at the time fixed for the completion of the research
project, the responsible research project leader will give a report to the client
on the work done including particulars of utilization of materials and employment of staff.

The "building practice" is given the opportunity to approach research institutes (by commissioning research tasks) or they may apply to the Ministry of
Building for inclusion of their tasks into a research programme.

For improved practical feedback in building research, the principle of responsibility on the part of the research teams is applied, which calls for a
demonstration of the practicability of solutions and for the teams' participation in the transfer of research and development results to industrial production or design. To facilitate that process, research establishments have
set up so-called "transfer teams", which include experienced practitioners
from the building industry (shop workers, production engineers, planners).

The Engineering Rationalization offices set up in various branches of the building industry have proved to be an important mechanism for transfer of technical
and scientific results of applied research.

The same idea is underlying the efforts of recent years to set up so-called
"application teams", particularly at universities, to systematically utilize
in technology the knowledge acquired in the field of mathematical and scientific fundamental research.

For a wide dissemination of the results of building research in the German
Democratic Republic the following informational measures are being taken:

- publication of catalogues and other informational material by
  the centralized Construction Information Office;

- organization of exhibitions in connection with specialists meetings;

- preparation of documentary films;

- organization of instruction courses for potential users.

In the German Democratic Republic the view is also held that it is a vitally
important question to avoid isolating technico-scientific development in building from the technico-scientific development in other similar branches (such
as machine building, vehicle construction, ship building, mining, etc.) and
likewise the promotion of the exchange of ideas with the research of these
branches.

For this purpose, use is made of interdisciplinary working groups of the
Research Council (which is linked to the Ministry of Science and Technology)
as well as of organizational links which exist between the Science and Technology Plans of the various Ministries and the Plan for Fundamental Research
of the Academy of Sciences and university institutes.

For important cross-sectional fields in the GDR there have been established
special research establishments of interbranch-character, such as the Institute
of Light Construction and Economic Use of Materials, the Institute of Welding
Engineering, the Central Station for Corrosion Protection, the Institute of
Labour Protection, etc. With these institutes, the establishments of building
research have set up a close working partnership. The links mentioned and
various other links to institutes of the Academy of Sciences offer a good
means of counterbalancing all tendencies of establishing a branch-specific
"scientific" standard in building research.

STAFFING

As stated above, long-term development of building research potentials (i.e.
research staff, scientific equipment and experimental facilities, information
system) is achieved by shaping the fields of research mentioned. The Ministry
of Building attaches great importance to the development of the potentials
of the Academy of Building or those of the major institutes in combines and
associations of enterprises as well as civil engineering colleges along the
lines of unified concepts formulated by the building research policy of the
German Democratic Republic.

Efforts are being made to adopt an approach to simultaneously linking the
development of staff for solutions to long-term tasks with the training of
a certain proportion of staff for short-term and medium-term tasks. The advantage of this approach is that the short-term tasks may be accomplished at
a higher standard using better equipment, while long-term research gets a
continual feedback to practice.

Systematic continuing education of research staff is considered to be a task
of a permanent nature. Form and content of continuing education depend on the
respective needs and requirements (training of users, sharing of practical
experience, upgrading of theoretical professional knowledge, communication of
knowledge of economic and socio-political contexts).

The Academy of Building has a special Centre for Continuing Education open to
staff of all research and development establishments of the building sector.
Colleges of technology and universities also provide continuing education
for the research staff of the building sector. The participation of qualified
building research workers in interdisciplinary specialists seminars held at
colleges, universities and the Academy of Sciences has proved successful.
These seminars are held on scientific and technical problems and problems of
human sciences (such as reliability of structures, cybernetic problems of the
design process, problems of man in relation to his environment in socialist
society).

Postgraduate continuing education for building research staff is provided by
colleges and will, in future, be available at the Centre of Continuing
Education of the Academy of Building.

In the building sector of our country, efforts are being made to base selection and training of research staff on the following principles:

- --the tendency to practicalism in building research should be overcome
  through the systematic raising of qualification, or through replacement
  of research workers;

- excessive specialization of staff is undesirable precisely because of the
  complexity of building research;

- specific tasks, calling for a high degree of theoretical specialization,
  will be dealt with in collaboration with institutes of the Academy of
  Sciences and with university institutes.

The close co-operation, planned by the Government, between the fundamental research conducted at colleges and universities and applied research of the building sector contributes to the fact that research at universities and colleges also gets some practical orientation.

The following mechanisms are currently used in the German Democratic Republic to improve the status of the research worker in the building sector and also as an incentive to higher output of research results:

- Moral and administrative support to progressive researchers and definite promotion of innovators at all levels of scientific and technological activities.

- A large-scale promotion programme aimed at the personal and professional career development of research workers primarily by providing training courses, postgraduate diploma and degree courses and by offering possibilities of self-realization and creative work in science and teaching, etc.

- Differential application of material incentives, primarily of bonuses paid in socialist competition and also of state prizes given for outstanding achievements in the field of science and science management.

Special attention is paid to the training of younger talented researchers and to their development aimed at their eventual promotion to a senior management level.

FINANCING

Twelve per cent of the state-run research is financed from the state budget (the Planning Commission of the GDR will decide on the amount of these funds). The rest is financed from a central fund, to which nationally owned enterprises contribute in proportion to their value of production (the Ministry of Building will decide on these funds as well).

In addition, enterprises may finance research which they directly assign to research institutes on a contract basis.

The total funds for research, as well as the research potential, are harmonized by the centralized state planning authorities. Thus, the traditionally small amount of research funds as compared to the production value of the building sector may be increased systematically in the course of further industrialization of building.

Thus, funds for research and development in the building sector in the German Democratic Republic are provided from two sources. For the most part, research tasks will be financed by enterprises, i.e. the firms will finance their own research and development facilities (if there are any). On the other hand, they will also act as clients, assigning research tasks on a contract basis to research and development establishments such as the Academy of Building and colleges.

As a rule, the Ministry of Building (or some other governmental body) will provide funds for tasks which are of vital importance to GDR's building sector as a whole (such as development of a new housing construction system using prefabricated large panels, subjects of fundamental research, etc.)

The principle of project-oriented funding is applied to ensure the elaboration of tasks of community interest by the research and development establishments at different levels.

It is quite obvious that construction enterprises would rather concentrate their efforts on such tasks which will yield short-term economic effects in terms of production output. Therefore the Ministry of Building promotes those research tasks which will, in the long run, increase efficiency of the construction industry.

Optimal proportions to be adhered to in the utilization of the research potential for short-term and/or long-term tasks is considered to an essential question in planning research and development capacities. Definite criteria for establishing optimal proportions have, however, not been found.

The total research and development expenditure in the building sector will increase to the extent as the level of industrialization of building and the quality requirements to be met by structures will be raised. In the German Democratic Republic building research expenditure currently amounts to 1.3 per cent of the value of production.

This figure is, however, of somewhat restricted validity because of uneven development of prices in different branches of the industry (including the prices for research output). In addition, it must be mentioned here that in the German Democratic Republic certain development capacities in the design field are not incorporated in the building research potential proper, but they are rather a part of the potential of construction engineering design.

The Federal Republic of Germany

In the Federal Republic of Germany, building research is conducted at numerous universities and institutes of technology, private, semi-state and state institutes as well as at industry research institutes. In addition, there are many individual experts who work regularly or occasionally in the field of building research. A catalogue listing all building research institutes comprises approximately 600 places working in this area.

There are many sponsors of building research that do not deal with the development of individual products or processes. Among them are Federal and State Ministries, corporate bodies including universities, working groups, foundations and corporations, housing industry, associations of the building industry and the building material industry, professional associations, trade unions, etc. Altogether there are about eighty institutions that promote research almost all of which are united in the "Working Group on Building Research" ("Arbeitsgemeinschaft für Bauforschung" (AGB)).

Thus it is clear that the structure of building research is greatly diversified in the Federal Republic of Germany.

STAFFING

Each body conducting research has complete freedom of decision as to the placing of research assignments. For greater clarity and a better co-ordination of the resulting manifold research activities, those bodies have teamed up in the "Arbeitsgemeinschaft für Bauforschung" on a voluntary basis.

Currently the AGB has seventy-one members. Their most important tasks are the following:

- Collecting and revising all news about research activities in buildings.
- Publishing all news about current and accomplished building research projects.
- Advising members of intended research projects.
- Collecting and revising foreign research works, as far as they are of interest to the building research in the Federal Republic of Germany.
- Consultation about problems of co-ordination, financing and publication.
- Consultation about problems of goals, priorities, development of research programmes.
- Expertise about research projects which have been submitted to members of

the "Arbeitsgemeinschaft für Bauforschung."

Among the activities of the "Arbeitsgemeinschaft" are building planning, structural engineering (including constructional physics) and building industry, whereby basic research, applied research and development research are given equal treatment. Research projects and regional planning, however, do not fall under the activities of the "Arbeitsgemeinschaft für Bauforschung".

Bodies of the AGB:

- Assembly of Members (making all major decisions about the work and its organization).

- Research Council (dealing in particular with goals and systematics of the building research as well as desirable orders of priority).

- Expert Working Groups (they are mainly to discuss projects submitted to members of the "Arbeitsgemeinschaft für Bauforschung"; furthermore, they also formulate research priorities within their field of activities).

The offices of the AGB are situated in the Federal Ministry for Regional Planning, Building and Urban Development (5300 Bonn-Bad Godesberg, Deichmanns Aue). The Federal Minister in office is at the same time chairman of the Working Group.

So far, emphasis in our activities has been on the edition of bulletins. These bulletins report on all current and accomplished building research projects. Thus, since 1971, about 2500 research activities of the Federal Republic of Germany and 500 of foreign countries have been recorded.

FINANCING

In the Federal Republic of Germany, the financing of building research corresponds to its diversified structure: the means for building research come from numerous sources. There are, however, no exact data available. According to an estimate of the year 1972, 140 million Deutschemarks have been spent for building research in our country. Roughly, the distribution of these funds is as follows:

- public sector (including universities)   27 per cent
- foundations, economic and professional associations 20 per cent
- industry research and development   53 per cent

PROSPECTS

In spite of the diversified structure of building research and the freedom of decision of all the numerous bodies concerned with building research, building research in our country is quite open. All building research activities are made known to all people concerned and thus a good information flow on a voluntary basis is made possible. Foreign research activities are increasingly being included in this programme. Thus, researchers of the Federal Republic of Germany are put in contact with their foreign colleagues working on similar problems.

CIB: Building Research Policies and
Sponsorship of Research

At the CIB Congress in Budapest in 1974, one session was devoted to the subject of Sponsorship of Research, and this mainly dealt with the experience of those engaged in research in obtaining funds for their work and the associated conditions which had to be met. The various arrangements reported reflected many variations in overall building research policies and in their implementation and also covered work of research groups in different situations - research institutes, universities, professional practice, industry or government, and market or centrally planned economy. It was thought that the discussion which developed, essentially reflecting the views of the various research groups concerned, could provide useful information for those considering building research policies; one of the main policy aims must be to ensure a research environment in which good work will flourish. The contributory papers and a report of the discussions have been published and provide considerable detail, but here it is perhaps more appropriate to concentrate on a summary of some of the main conclusions.

The session dealing with the sponsorship of reseach essentially provided a forum for exchange of experience and views about different methods of sponsorship and how these worked in practice. There were many differences in the detailed arrangements under which research was conducted but two main types of arrangements were clear.

Firstly, there was research which was financed under long-term grants and secondly, research conducted under short-term contracts. Although there were some institutes which worked almost entirely on long-term grants - mainly national institutes - most institutes obtained an appreciable proportion of their finance from shorter-term contracts, and one national research institute in fact financed some two-thirds of its work in this way.

A wide variety of arrangements was covered in the discussion as members discussed their experience. In fact what appeared was that, although certain qualifications and criticisms were made, most of the arrangements reported could be made to work. A key factor in a successful arrangement appeared to be the need for good communication between those sponsoring the research and those conducting the research. Major difficulties had risen in the past and it was suggested that these had often been due to poor communication. Clearly it was worthwhile spending a considerable effort to ensure that the sponsor knew what he would get so far as results were concerned; then he should be encouraged to become deeply involved in the progress of the work - it might even be possible to make a representative of the sponsor feel he was a member of the team. It was also very important that the research worker did not simply pass the results to the sponsor but that he also assisted in further application into practice.

Members suggested that with such arrangements research workers could get a high level of job satisfaction even when their work was essentially a series of short-term contracts. This might not apply to all research workers but there were many who could enjoy such work. We discussed the problem of ensuring the continuity of work for small research teams working under short-term contracts - they sometimes saw funds for their current contract running out as their contract came to completion, and had the problem of ensuring a new contract so that the team could be kept together. We did not find the same difficulty in phasing work where multiple teams were conducting parallel short-term contracts in a larger group, although even there difficulties could arise if specialized staff had to be recruited for a particular contract - there were first of all possible delays in recruiting and also when the work was completed there might not be further suitable work available for a specialist.

We also discussed what appears to be a developing pattern in a number of European countries so far as government-sponsored research is concerned. This involves starting by defining aims and goals of research and within these setting down objectives for research. Programmes of research are then worked up to meet these objectives or possibly derived objectives. It was thought that this approach might well be used not only by governments but also by research institutes financed by overall grants - the same type of examination could then be conducted within the institute.

The above summary deals with some of the major conclusions developed at the Congress. Many other topics affecting the conduct of work in research units were included in the original papers by members, and these were summarized in an overall review paper presented at the Congress (Ref: *CIB Congress Proceedings*, Vol. 1/2, pp. 525-531). Many of the topics listed are very relevant to the development of building research policies.

Netherlands

The building industry should itself ensure that a balanced flow of funds is available for R&D. It is desirable that this activity be promoted through governmental support or statutory regulations.

The building industry should create, as and when expedient jointly with the appropriate national authorities, an institution or agency that controls the monies concerned and which ensures that, in respect of those funds, R&D is performed whose results are generally of interest to the building world.

For the programming, initiation and "keeping in the right track" of R&D activities, co-operation of experts from actual building practice is indispensable. Accordingly, organizing procedures aiming at such co-operation should be agreed.

Inherent in the organization of R&D thus financed, it will be of significance to have the research workers supported by a small committee of people "with both feet in actual building practice". This is to ensure that R&D yields results which can indeed be used in practice, and that adequate attention is paid to content and manner of knowledge transfer in the final stage. Active governmental participation in making pertinent arrangements is desirable.

A research organization should earn part of its cost by demonstrating its value in advisory activities.

The greater proportion of the research workers should therefore couple their major task of carrying out R&D appropriate to the organization with a more or less subsidiary involvement in industrial or other practical problems, in an advisory role.

Each research organization should contain within it some experts with a broad, visionary, "helicopter-type" approach to the field of building R&D in order to safeguard the integrated and multi-disciplinary nature of the work being done.

The mobility of R&D staff and personnel, in terms of detailing or switching to industry and back, should be encouraged.

F

Sweden

The present organization of research is characterized by an abundant differentiation according to traditional subject areas. Higher education follows this traditional division into disciplines, although efforts have been made to establish interdisciplinary co-operative organizations. A great deal of research at university level is financed by grants from unidisciplinary research councils, such as the Council for Social Science Research and the Council for Research in the Natural Sciences.

In recent years a growing number of specific research institutes have been set up in various sectors. The National Institute for Building Research and the Institute for Social Research are two such examples.

In this way research organization has become very extensive and somewhat confusing. Special bodies have therefore been set up in recent years for the co-ordination and planning of research in various sectors.

The Swedish Council for Building Research has the task of observing research and rationalization needs within the building and construction sector and of distributing grants towards research and experimentation in the sector in response to those needs. The Council is not empowered to engage directly in research, but its duty is to ensure that the activities financed by its grants are duly publicized.

The financial support given by the Council to R&D is itself financed by a building research charge, to which is geared a special state grant, and also by state grants earmarked for R&D and experimental building within the energy sector. At present the building research charge is 0.7 per cent of payrolls in the building and construction sector.

Research and development expenditure in the Swedish building sector during 1973/4 totalled some Skr 200 million. Roughly one-fifth of this expenditure was financed by the Council, the remainder by contractors, the building material industry, public authorities, clients, consultants and others. It would seem, however, as though the portion of activities financed by the Council has greatly increased.

R&D financed by the building sector itself has declined in volume during the past few years. This is regrettable for several reasons. Large proprietary, administrative and commissioning organizations within the building sector are often very well placed for the conduct of research and development activities, and the council intends to take various measures of a general nature to support the stagnant R&D activities of the entrepreneurial sector.

In order to play an active part in the development of the building industry, research must be closely allied with the bodies responsible for development activities. (A response paper on Subject B from the Associated General Contractors and House-builders of Sweden (SBEF) describes how co-operation has been established between research and development in two problem areas — road and street construction and rock construction technology.)

The expansion of building research beyond the purely technical aspects of building to include social, economic and ecological aspects as well as energy questions calls for an interdisciplinary approach. This approach involves many unsolved problems. Experience accruing from Swedish building research has also confirmed that there are considerable problems to be overcome and that postgraduate recruitment is currently the main impediment to the development of an interdisciplinary approach in this sector. More recently, however, there have been signs of change in postgraduate studies, the composition of research groups and the development of research environments calculated to improve the situation. (These tendencies have been described in a response paper on Subject B presented by Carin Boalt, page 146).

The Swedish Council for Building Research is confronted with something of a new situation where the organization of research is concerned. In the course of its future activities, the Council intends to develop a more decentralized system which will foster direct contacts between R&D interests and researchers. The emphasis of the Council's duties will be more upon the conduct of general R&D planning, the articulation of financial needs and the distribution of research finance.

THE SWEDISH BUILDING INDUSTRY AND BUILDING RESEARCH[*]

SBEF, the Associated General Contractors and House-builders of Sweden,[**] has for some years been pursuing research and development activities in a number of concrete problem areas, viz. road and street construction and rock construction technology. This work is being done in specially constituted liaison groups in which the recipients of R&D results are widely represented. The purpose of this work is

(a)　to cater for the need for production-oriented R&D,

(b)　to utilize the suggestions and ideas occurring in the building industry with regard to R&D projects.

The following outline of the activities of the two groups will serve to illustrate how a direct link between production and R&D can result in more concretely guided and demand-controlled building research.

---

[*]　Compiled by Bertil Grandinsson, The Associated General Contractors and House-builders of Sweden.

[**]　SBEF, the representative organization of the Swedish building industry, has 215 affiliated firms with a combined personnel strength of 60,000 and a turnover of Skr 16,000 million.

The Road Research Group

The SBEF Road Research Group includes representatives of road administrators, producers and researchers. The group initiates and conducts production-oriented R&D projects in the streets and roads sector, financed by the Swedish Council for Building Research. An allocation of Skr 700,000 has been made for the fiscal year 1977/8.

The tasks of the group include the inventory of R&D requirements among clients and producers, the administration of current R&D projects and the maintenance of contact with R&D in progress elsewhere in the street and road construction sector. R&D results are publicized in the form of reports and articles and at specially arranged conferences.

Current projects include "The use of geomembranes in transport routes", "Lime stabilization of poor-quality substrata", "Production of asphalt compound in drum mixers", "Road surfacing and asphalt emulsion concrete".

The Rock Construction Research Group

Together with the mining industry, explosives manufacturers, building clients and rock technology consultants, SBEF has founded the Swedish Rock Mechanics Research Foundation, BeFo, whose basic activities are 60 per cent financed by industry and 40 per cent by the State. In addition the Foundation receives certain grants from the Swedish Council for Building Research towards projects of particular relevance to building. At present BeFo's total R&D budget balances at Skr 2 million per annum. SBEF's contributions towards BeFo's activities are channelled through a Rock Construction Research Group including representatives of member companies engaged in this sector.

The group surveys the needs of the building industry for R&D in rock mechanics and endeavours to respond to the needs thus ascertained by initiating important projects, primarily under the aegis of BeFo. The group is represented in reference groups for BeFo projects and also endeavours to influence R&D activities conducted by other bodies in the field of rock mechanics. Another important task of the group is to inform building companies of the results of current and completed rock mechanics projects; for example, an annual information Day is held for this purpose.

Recent projects involving the Rock Construction Research Group have included the following:

"Grouting materials and methods",

"Demands for better and safer underground ventilation in tunnelling",

"The span and geometrical design of large rock storage facilities",

"Full-face tunnelling",

"Mechanical scrapping".

Conclusions

Activities in the two R&D groups have shown that the organization of research on these lines can have many advantages, including the following:

The close demarcation of a R&D area makes it easy to locate transmitters of ideas and recipients of findings within individual firms.

The interested parties are involved in R&D activities and feel responsible for them.

The continuity of the activities helps gradually to establish good R&D environments.

Contacts between researchers and industry are encouraged.

The group representing the recipients of R&D results feels responsible for information.

Similar advantages should accrue from the organization of R&D activities in other building sectors on the same lines as in the two SBEF research groups. The resultant closer involvement of industry in building research should play an active part in bringing building research and the building industry closer together.

THE TRAINING OF BUILDING RESEARCHERS[*]

The introductory reports on Subject B (by Mr. Kunszt, Hungary, and Mr. O. Eriksson, Sweden) emphasize the importance of access to

- adequately trained researchers who can tackle the problems of building research on an interdisciplinary or multidisciplinary basis,
- research environments conducive to creativity and innovation and providing abundant contacts with reality and a disposition to steer research findings towards application.

Both writers put great emphasis on the obstacles presented by the traditional academic world in the majority of countries.

Experience of Swedish research in the man-made environment sector confirms that there are considerable problems involved and that researcher recruitment is a bottleneck in the development of this research sector.

Recently, however, there have been clear tendencies towards a transformation of research training, constellations of research teams and the development of research environments calculated to improve the situation. Here are some of the tendencies in brief.

More and more academic disciplines have developed a growing interest in the system of man and environment. Formerly building research was primarily based on technical, production-oriented disciplines, but today questions concerning man and the environment are being studied in several disciplines, e.g. sociology, psychology, social anthropology and comparative ethnology.

Building research was formerly dominated by spot studies of an empirical

---

[*] By Professor Carin Boalt, the Faculty of Technology in the University of Lund.

character. Demands are now evolving for the development of general theory
and the co-ordination of projects within common frames of reference.

The formerly highly specialized and individualized studies for postgraduate
degrees are now being replaced by opportunities of studying across disciplinary and faculty boundaries and working in teams with a view, for example,
to the presentation of doctoral theses. This will reduce the risk, referred to by both Kunszt and Eriksson, of inflexibility in the academic system, e.g. the predominance of specialist professors.

There is an increasing tendency in favour of types of problem whose treatment
is aimed at producing changes in the processes connected with the planning,
construction, administration and use of the built-up environment. Examples
of this kind include interdisciplinary projects on resource conservation in
building, on the design of work environments and on the renovation of old
buildings. This in turn demands training in methods of applied research.

Efforts are being made to internationalize training and research. In the
building sector this is reflected, for example, by the interest taken in
problems connected with social and technological change in the developing
countries. Previously there has been a tendency (especially in the building industry sector) for the technologies of the affluent countries to be
transferred to the developing countries. There is now a growing realization that greater consideration must be given to local, cultural, economic
and technical conditions. This realization should characterize educational
co-operation between affluent and developing countries.

The following are some of the difficulties which have been encountered in
Sweden when training researchers to adopt an interdisciplinary approach to research problems:

Difficulties in understanding and assimilating theoretical instruction, concepts and methods in different disciplines.

Lack of research tradition and research environments in faculties of architecture and engineering, for example.

A tendency to set up research teams without first checking to see that the
researchers have progressed far enough in their own research training. In
many cases this has led to projects which have been relatively amateurish
and untheoretical.

The danger of the members of a team who have scientific backgrounds and training predominating over those who have had practical experience and those who
are concerned with applied aspects. A careful study must therefore be made
of the allocation of roles and responsibilities within a project.

If researchers come from different institutions, the institutional management
— usually the professor of the subject concerned — must accept and partici-
page in the broadening of the traditional subject which may result. A professor of psychology, for example, should realize the possibility of studies
developing in architectural psychology.

Grants are usually awarded for limited projects which are conducted and then
reported. This makes it hard to establish continuity and a successive development of environments for interdisciplinary research.

It will be interesting to see how prominent these problems are in other countries, what means have been devised of solving them and what advantages can be
expected from international co-operation on the training of interdisciplinary
research and a greater volume of research exchange in connection with current
research projects.

DISSEMINATION OF INFORMATION AND UTILIZATION OF RESEARCH RESULTS

The Federal Republic of Germany

GENERAL REMARKS

The problems of putting research results relating to structural engineering effectively into practice are very complex. Building research is necessarily intended for many people and institutions with different forms of organization and different terms of reference who, because of this fact, must be approached in different ways. The structure of the building sector itself has an inhibiting effect on innovation in many fields so that the problem of putting research findings into practice turns into a problem of putting them through. Innovative activities are to a large extent left to voluntary initiatives. Innovation is in itself a very lengthy process, and as its effect is always partial, verifying its success is extremely difficult and fraught with uncertainty.

In general, reports are made on the majority of building research projects carried out in the Federal Republic of Germany. Many findings are published — either in a complete or in an abridged version — by the sponsoring institutions or the research stations in their own series of publications or as articles in technical journals. In addition to this, information on particular research results may be disseminated in seminars, lectures and conferences, demonstration films or put into practice in demonstration projects.

Thus, sufficient information on all research results is indeed available to the professional circles. If the problem of information transfer exists nevertheless, this is due, on the one hand, to a lack of information need and a certain resistance to innovation prevailing in broad sections of the building industry, and on the other hand, it is due to the flood of information which actually leads to a surfeit.

EXPERIENCE SO FAR

When research programmes are made, focal points of research determined and research projects in the field of structural engineering carried out, the professional circles are in a position to follow the whole process and it is carried out with their support.

Research is related to practice already when selecting the research subjects, namely by

- public invitations to tender and by directly approaching all building research institutes and individual researchers;

- public discussion of the applications submitted in the expert study groups of the Working Group on Building Research (Arbeitsgemeinschaft für

Bauforschung (AGB)), which consist of scientists and researchers and representatives of the building industry, of public authorities and of the users;

- collaboration with the expert study groups in determining the focal points
  of research;

- requesting applicants to make proposals as to how to enable a rapid application of the research results.

While the research works are in progress, the link with the practice is maintained by

- providing continuous guidance for research projects by an independent
  study group;

- drawing attention to existing documentation centres and obliging researchers to inform themselves on the "state of the art";

- submitting final reports ready for publication and short summary reports.

A number of research results are made available to the standardization committees and other bodies; they are directly incorporated into building standards,
guidelines and regulations.

Research results are directly applied, tested and demonstrated to experts within the framework of the joint building programme of the Federal Government and
the States, e.g. by means of experimental and comparative building projects.

Final reports on the results of building research are published in series of
publications, technical journals and books. Another means to publish research
activities are the bulletins issued by the Working Group on Building Research
(AGB) which comprises about 70 institutions concerned with research promotion.
In these bulletins, each research project is presented stating the subject of
research, the names and addresses of the sponsor and the researcher, in what
form the research report is to be published, and giving a short summary of the
goals and/or the most important findings. Since the Working Group was founded
in 1969, more than 2,500 research projects have been published. Most interested in these research bulletins are the members of the Working Group, other
experts and above all technical journalists. Many technical journals borrow
information from these bulletins which is of particular interest to their read-
ers.

There can be no doubt about the fact that almost all results and findings of
the building research are eventually reflected in the practice of building.
However, this often takes place with a considerable time lag, as the building
industry often shows a strong inclination to stick to old habits and to accept
innovations only reluctantly. Therefore, it is difficult to check whether the
dissemination of individual research results has been successful. What can be
done, however, is to watch developments in individual fields of study and to
estimate the influence of scientific building research.

The prospects of a successful application of building research results are relatively good when they are translated into building standards, administrative
guidelines, regulations etc. This is why fewer difficulties arise in the field
of research concerned with materials and products, in so far as new findings
are directly disseminated by means of standards set up by and general approvals
issued by the building authorities.

For the purpose of disseminating research findings relevant to rationalization, the Federal Ministry for Regional Planning, Building and Urban Development has published a "rationalization catalogue". The Federal government's guidelines for the allocation of funds for low-income housing ("Social Housing Scheme") - and partly the State's corresponding assistance guidelines as well - which constitute a regulatory framework have already been revised on the basis of this catalogue.

As to the fields of thermal and sound insulation, protection against humidity and indoor climate, one had to start from scratch, so to speak, after 1945. The use of new building materials and — in comparison to pre-war times — lighter construction types on the one hand and the demand for improved quality and increased production of housing on the other, raised a large number of questions relating to constructional physics which could only be solved by considerably intensifying research efforts in this field.

Since 1960, the research efforts in the field of prefabricated construction have been intensified. Besides the research on materials and the development of new calculating methods, comparative studies on various building systems were carried out as well as surveys in the form of catalogues and economic studies on the building industry.

An important example of this is the so-called "Prefab Houses Catalogue", which contributed to providing whoever is interested with an impartial overview of the manifold supply and to enabling objective decisions. At the same time, it contributed to improving the "quality awareness" among the producers.

Experience has shown that experts by and large are less interested in reports on individual research projects than in crosscut reports covering a self-contained field of study and rather longer periods of time. Thus, priority is to be given to promoting such crosscut reports. However, it is very difficult to find researchers who are qualified for as well as willing to carry out this work, because for most of them it offers too little opportunity to show their ability while requiring relatively much working effort.

A CONCEPT FOR THE YEARS TO COME

The Research Council of the Working Group on Building Research (AGB) has submitted a number of proposals for the application of research results, establishing the following order of importance:

- organization of information seminars on research results of particular importance to be passed on to a large number of people interested in them;

- binding agreements between the Federal Ministry for Regional Planning, Building and Urban Development and as many technical journals as possible with a view to establishing regular columns on building research;

- introduction of a supply of information on research reports graded according to the users' information needs;

- preferential information on research results which have already been put to the test or even put into practice;

- activation of information policy by regularly publishing special press releases on building research:

- making research commissions dependent on binding conditions as to the kind of language to be used for the research reports and their construction;

- regular publication of supplements to the bulletins of federations and associations as well as technical journals to be used e.g. for loose-leaf editions;

- prescription of a uniform presentation of typescripts for research reports which would improve their legibility;

- intensified promotion of demonstration projects;

- promotion of all possible ways and means of further education.

Netherlands

A policy should be built up which enables decisions to be made continuously as to the type of knowledge and information that is to be offered to, or acquired by, each individual level of the various parties concerned in building. The appropriate points of time should be specified, too. The above does not apply to R&D results only; it also relates to knowledge and information previously available whose topicality increases through altered conditions.

The accessibility to available knowledge and information should be promoted.

The desired type and content of pertinent publications, audio-visual means, etc. should be tailored to the target-groups concerned. An institution or agency capable of implementing these activities should be created.

Dissemination of knowledge and information should be rendered as effective as possible through adequate feedback.

In the transfer of knowledge and information, standardization plays a significant part in that its application creates the necessity for all concerned in building, to familiarize themselves with at least the essence of R&D results underpinning its specifications.

The building field is subject to so many changes that post-graduate courses, etc., are a must for all those concerned, throughout their career in building.

Communication with present and future users is a point calling for attention, too.

Sweden

National and international building regulations are an important channel for the communication of research results to the building process. (See also response paper on Subject C from the National Board of Urban Planning, p. 152.) This channel has been very useful in a period when industrialization as such has constituted an important goal of development in the building sector, and building regulations will in future continue to be an important channel of information from building research.

The phase of development which has now been entered by Sweden and various other countries is characterized by demands for greater user influence in the planning, construction and administration of the built-up environment. This new tendency calls for greater efforts towards the dissemination of research results. The users of buildings do not have the qualifications and resources of public authorities, clients and the building industry to receive and process the information required for active participation in the building process.

Close attention will have to be given to the task of giving users the information they need at the very moment when they need it. (See also response paper on Subject C by Olof Eriksson, p. 160.)

Thus building research has a very wide and variegated range of interests to cater for. One thing which all these interests have in common is limited time and capacity for the receipt of information. Moreover, their need of information seldom coincides with the presentation of research results. Besides, research results are only a part of the documentation which is needed in connection with development work, etc. This makes it necessary for information to be communicated at the recipient's initiative, and at the time when he is prepared to receive information and use it. (See also response paper by A.S. Stern on Subject C, p. 156.)

Wider international co-operation is needed concerning the interchange of information on research results. One or more documentation centres should be established in each country, and information should be exchanged between them. (See also response paper by A.S. Stern on Subject C.)

THE DISSEMINATION OF RESEARCH RESULTS — A SERVICE TO THE RECIPIENT*

The question is: which needs do we want to satisfy by disseminating research results:

- the recipient's need of information?
- the researcher's need to promote his research?
- or the administrator's need to justify the funds spent?

Assuming it is the recipient of research we want to help, let us regard the situation from his point of view.

The recipients of research results are:

- other research workers,
- practitioners,
- politicians and the general public.

What they have in common is a limited amount of time and a limited capacity to assimilate new knowledge, at the same time as there are many "transmitters" competing for their attention. And it is their attention we want.

In determining the efficacy with which research results are disseminated, let us not be misled by false indicators such as the number of copies sold. We can always increase the number of copies distributed by decreasing the price or by giving them away, but will more of them be read?

The cost of one copy of a published report in Sweden is about 50 kronor. The cost of reading it during working hours is about 1000 kronor. It is therefore important for the recipient to read the "right" material.

The studies made at Byggdok indicate that the following should be considered in order to "get across" to the reader:

- The point in time when information is requested does not usually coincide with the point in time when research results are being disseminated.
- The information offered in the research report usually forms only a part of the information requested and has to be supplemented from other sources.
- Often the form and language of the research report do not coincide with the ability, the wishes and the expectations of the recipient.

This shows that responsibility for the information transfer is gradually to be shifted from the "sender" to the "receiver", who initiates the process at a time when he needs the knowledge and is ready to receive it.

He must, of course, be made aware of his information needs and the possibilities of satisfying them by a very selective and readily understandable stream of information from the sender. In this connection the role of periodical journals should not be underestimated.

---

*   By A.S. Stern, the Swedish Institute of Building Documentation (Byggdok).

As stated in the introductory report, the possibilities of personal contact between the recipient and the research worker are very limited. This is what makes it necessary to regard what has been done and can be done in order to improve the utilization of research results.

In the early fifties we had an intensive discussion concerning a classification system for the building industry. The underlying assumption was that once we had such a system the problem of dissemination would be solved by a distribution system in which everybody subscribed to the information he was interested in. Today we still lack a good classification system, but even if we had one, none of the basic problems would be solved by improved distribution alone.

What has happened in the meantime is that a new technology has been developed, enabling us to search remote data-bases in an interactive way from relatively inexpensive computer terminals (US $200 approx.).

Many other sciences are already making extensive use of this possibility. It is an imperative task for building research to create an international data-base for building science. No time should be lost, for there are many difficulties to overcome. An arrangement of this kind will enable us to store information when it becomes available and to produce it when it is requested.

The recipients, however, will also need guidance and service in order to be able to search, select and compile — they will need an interface, a link between themselves and research. This kind of service can be provided by national documentation centres as proposed by the ECE Conference in Geneva in 1949.[*] Another important task of international co-operation will be to stimulate the establishment of such national centres.

In Sweden we have such a centre — created and sponsored by the National Council for Building Research (BFR). The experience gained during the 10 years it has been operative proves that it can be run successfully to the benefit of all concerned.

It must not be confused with libraries conserving knowledge for future generations or with the sales promotion activities of building material producers. In order to function as a useful and impartial service, it must be able to attract qualified personnel possessing subject knowledge and practicel experience.

Given the wholehearted support of research administrators, it is possible to recruit competent people — practitioners and research workers. This work offers direct contact with the recipients and, given due recognition and appreciation, is both challenging and stimulating.

---

[*] Proceedings of the Conference on Building Documentation E/ECE/111-E/ECE/HOU/BD/2, Geneva, November 1949.

DISSEMINATION OF INFORMATION AND UTILIZATION OF RESEARCH RESULTS*

Utilization of Research Results

Mr. D.A. Senior has stated in his paper that the ultimate beneficiary of building research and development is the general public which for the most part receives its benefits so to speak at second hand through the authorities which
promulgate technical requirements. The need for research and development in
connection with building regulations and codes has been recognized to an increased extent.

This is probably related to the fact that the authorities are aware of the need
to make extensive efforts towards modernization and co-ordination of regulations
and codes on the national level. The endeavour to make the regulations amenable
to innovations and to promote industrialization of the building process evident-
ly contribute to these efforts.

It should be emphasized as a general recommendation that it is very important
for building regulations with mandatory requirements on public health and safety
to be based on correct and reliable knowledge since these regulations, to a
greater extent than many other documents which can usually be applied in a less
restrictive manner, govern the design and construction of buildings.

In drawing up a programme for research and development regarding building regulations, it is naturally of primary importance to try and compile informations
on which human requirements with regard to housing and premises of work may be
based. These requirements should relate to the stability and strength of the
buildings and also their essential fundamental characteristics. The requirements must also be formulated in view of human reactions to noise, heat, cold,
air quality, etc., and be based on social and medical research. The conditions
and methods of verification associated with these requirements must also be
studied.

When requirements in building regulations are to be formulated, it is necessary
to weigh quality against economy. It is therefore also an essential duty of
research and development work on building regulations to study the economic consequences of different requirement levels.

In this connection we want to underline the need of a national philosophy of
security. Is safety in buildings well balanced with safety in traffic or with
the safety in common working situations? We think that the current hot debate
on the increase of atomic energy and the use of new chemicals will make it necessary for the politicians to formulate and implement one consistent theory of
security for the different fields of society's responsibility.

When building regulations are formulated or revised it is often found out that
the requirements in these regulations must be based on insufficient grounds,
owing to the fact that the information available is incomplete. The same may
also apply as regards the test and design methods used to verify these requirements. In order that these shortcomings in the necessary information may be
remedied, it is important that research and development requirements are noted
and handed over to the appropriate research institutions.

---

* Response paper submitted by the observers from the National Swedish Board
   of Physical Planning and Building.

In Sweden the central authority for building regulations has published a report on research and development needs in connection with building regulation work (FoU-behov för Svensk Byggnorm, Report No. 10 from the National Swedish Board of Physical Planning and Building). Two hundred items were listed under three orders of priority depending on urgency, resources and the degree to which research and development needs have been made explicit at present. The programme extends over the period 1971-5.

With the prospect of a new publication of a revised edition of Svensk Byggnorm (SNB 1975) the fact has been brought forward that about three-fourths of the FoU-behov stated had been investigated into more or less closely.

The favourable experiences resulted in an updated report on research and development needs in connection with building regulations in Svensk Byggnorm 1975 (SBN 1975) being worked out and the report will be published by the Swedish Council for Building Research.

Future co-operation between authorities and other institutions which are responsible for building regulations and other forms of building control, aimed at harmonization of the regulations, should for practical reasons be based on information and experience available in the countries taking part. The needs for research and development relating to future co-operation on building regulations should, however, be elucidated at the same time.

It is desirable that international organizations should co-operate in carrying out the research and development tasks which are of common interest to authorities responsible for building regulations. It is primarily CIB and RILEM which should participate in this work, but other international organizations which are engaged on scientific matters relating to the building sector, such as technology, medicine, sociology and economics, should also be interested in taking part. International cooperation may be organized regarding the physiological and psychological reaction of the human organism to the physical and social environment. Serious efforts have to be made with a view to feasible application of functional (or performance) requirements in building regulations. It is also urgent that the influence of data processing on the building industry and building regulations should be studied.

Dissemination of Information

In Sweden, as well as in the United Kingdom as Mr. D.A. Senior has reported in his paper, the building requirements firstly state an overall requirement in rather general terms, supplemented by quantified requirements or by recommendations of "deemed to satisfy" solutions.

The "deemed to satisfy" clauses in Sweden normally refer to Swedish standards. We want to underline what Mr. D.A. Senior has stated, namely that research results incorporated into regulations, codes and standards ensure their wide adoption and that this is a major way of introducing research results into practice.

In this connection Mr. D.A. Senior has stated that the requirements in British standards can tend towards those capable of achievement by the generality of the associated parts of the industry. The Swedish central authority for building regulations has noticed this question and in consequence given all "mandatory" requirements in the code and has not referred to standards in these requirements. Standards are the means for communications and rationalizations inside industry. But standards will not solve the problem of society which is to put requirements on industry to ensure that the citizen's need of safety, health and welfare are safeguarded. We can — and do so too — use the way of referring to standards in our official regulations when standards show the way to fulfil the regulation and in this way ensure that official regulations need not be overspecified and detailed. But we cannot go the opposite way and let standards replace regulations.

DISSEMINATION OF INFORMATION AND UTILIZATION OF RESEARCH RESULTS[*]

The model of industrialized building which has come to prevail during the decades that have elapsed since the end of the last war has involved a considerable degree of centralization. Industrial development has been taken to demand large production units and, accordingly, large projects and large sponsoring organizations. Uniform requirements concerning the results of the industrial process have been taken to constitute another precondition. This has led to a desire for uniform building regulations, first nationally and then internationally.

The current view is that, in order not to stand in the way of industrial development, building regulations should contain functional requirements instead of technical specifications. Building regulations should form a framework within which the process of industrial development can be given free rein. The necessary technical uniformity is obtained by means of standardization with a high degree of industrial influence.

This approach has made building regulations an important — perhaps the most important — channel whereby information can be communicated to the building process concerning the requirements which the results of the process — building development — must satisfy. This has been a rational arrangement during a period in which industrialization as such has been an important developmental target in the building sector.

The phase of development now being passed through in Sweden and other countries is characterized by a demand for greater participation and direct user influence in the planning, construction and administration of the built-up environment. User influence demands scope for action within the framework provided by the building regulations. If everything is regulated in detail, there will be nothing left for users to influence.

Thus industrialization and user influence both stand to benefit from building regulations being of an outline character. But they are also competitors for influence within the framework. Greater user influence causes functional demands to be directly communicated by users to the building process. Since they are not a generalization of research and are not filtered through the system of norms, these demands cannot be expected to be of a uniform nature. On the contrary, it is in their nature to vary from one group to another, and from one individual or region to another, according to socio-economic and cultural circumstances.

In the production/consumption of goods, this antithesis is resolved, at least in theory, by the mechanisms of the market. Individual needs are catered for by choosing between different goods produced in long runs. A certain restric-

---

[*] By Olof Eriksson, Swedish Council for Building Research.

tion of choice is counterbalanced by greater supply and lower prices. The mechanisms of the market cannot function on these lines in the building sector, because the freedom of choice available to users in that sector is limited by a number of factors — the great durability of the product, its geographical immobility and so on. Groups with limited spending power are never well provided for by the forces of the market. Users therefore have to be assured of direct influence on the planning-building-administration process if they are to be capable of securing the fulfilment of their own demands. The demands of the industrialization epoch for uniformity must take second place when they come into conflict with participatory goals.

The transformation described above demands greater efforts towards the dissemination of research results. The model of industrialized building incorporates three factors — public authorities, sponsors and the building industry — which have to be supplied with research results. All of these three are experts and have, or should have, resources of their own for the receipt and processing of information. The new main factor in a model of participatory demands — the users of the built-up environment — are not experts and do not possess resources of their own for the receipt and processing of information. Even if each individual user is an expert on his own situation, users need the support of research results in order to be able to assert their interests in relation to other principal actors. In a building process arranged for popular participation, the users should not receive less support from research than others.

Building research, therefore, cannot focus its dissemination of information solely on the three traditional main actors, adjusting its methods to their conditions and demands. The task of informing users about the things they need to know and exactly when they need to know them is probably much more difficult and must therefore be given a corresponding degree of consideration.

SOME FACTS ABOUT THE COUNCIL FOR BUILDING RESEARCH (BFR)

The task of the Swedish Council for Building Research — known in Sweden under the initials BFR — is to keep itself informed of the need for research and rationalization in the field of construction and civil engineering and on the basis of this to provide grants for research and experimental activities in these fields. The Council is not itself authorized to conduct research, but is empowered to disseminate in suitable ways the results of activities carried out with the financial support of the Council.

The Council falls under the Ministry of Housing. It has a board of eleven members appointed by the Government and representing different areas of interest within the activities of the Council.

The Council is assisted in its work of planning the allocation of grants and evaluating the results obtained by interim programme committees and groups. The Council's staff, divided into three sections — administration, a research secretariat and information — is responsible for day-to-day activities.

Research and development activities (R&D) sponsored by the Council are financed by means of a special tax and a supplementary government grant, as well as special grants allocated by the Government for R&D on energy and experimental construction related to the energy field. The special tax is equivalent

(May 1977) to 0.7 per cent of the salaries paid by employers in the construction and civil engineering sector.

CONSTRUCTION R&D IN SWEDEN — COMPARATIVE STATISTICS

Figure 1 illustrates the extent of all research and development in construction (byggFoU) in Sweden, expressed in million Sw.kr., 1970 monetary values. These figures are based on a limited statistical survey of all R&D activities in the building sector during the period 1970/1 and 1973/4. During both these periods about one-fifth of all activities were financed by BFR. In current prices this share represents 40 and 45 million Sw.kr. respectively (see table under Fig. 1). Comparative figures for 1976/7 and 1977/8 are 102 and 145 million Sw.kr. respectively.

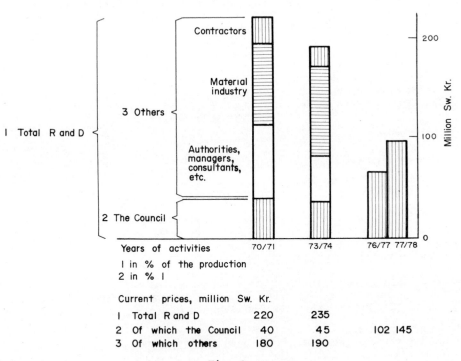

Fig. 1

THE ACTIVITIES OF BFR — ITS BUDGET AND OBJECTIVES

The budget for BFR activities, in current prices for the financial years 1974/5 to 1976/7 monetary values of the period 1977/8 to 1980/1, is presented in Figure 2 in which the actual budget up and until the year 1977/8 is given, while the figures for the period after this date represent envisaged but not yet approved activities (May 1977). Energy-oriented R&D activities (EFoU) according to a special Riksdag decision, energy-oriented prototype and demonstration projects (EPD) directed to the trimming of central heating plants and Local Authority energy planning, as well as research-oriented experimental construction in the energy field (FExpE) are shown separately from general research and development activities (AFoU) sponsored by BFR.

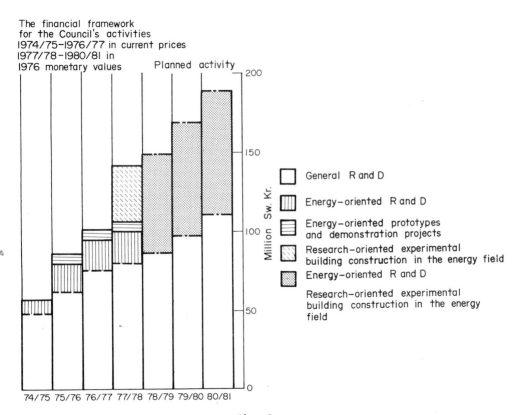

Fig. 2

PERSONS WORKING IN R&D SUPPORTED BY BFR GRANTS

Figure 3 illustrates the different categories of researchers working with the aid of grants from BFR. In all about 400 to 500 persons at universities and institutes of technology are employed on research projects supported by BFR. The large number of researchers in comparison to the size of the BFR grants is explained by the supplementary resources provided by the universities and institutes of technology. Other researcher categories, i.e. research institutes and special bodies, account for a similar number, with the National Institute for Building Research (SIB) in Gävle, the largest building research institute in the country, accounting for the largest number followed by authorities, building sector research bodies, property owners and property managers, construction and building material companies, consultants and finally individual researchers.

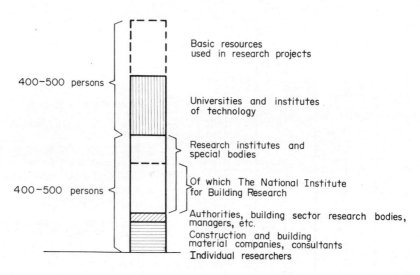

Who does R and D sponsored by the Swedish Council for Building Research ?

Fig. 3

INTERNATIONAL COLLABORATION

The Federal Republic of Germany

It is only by means of a systematic effort both by science and research on an international level that building can be developed to the extent that it complies with the standards of our civilization and technology. People in all countries and beyond frontiers must be able to benefit from findings in the field of building research. The comprehensive scientific and technical interlacing suggests an international collaboration.

As to the international collaboration, real progress has been made during the past years, not only in many fields of building research but also through effective measures. On many levels there is an exchange of experience with other countries about research projects and research results in building. In the Federal Republic of Germany numerous bodies conducting research, research institutes, individual researchers, special associations, etc., take part in this exchange of experience. They work actively in international organizations such as ECE, UEAtc, CIB, ISO, CEN, RILEM, FIP, etc., for example in the fields of harmonization of building regulations and of the international measurement co-ordination (modular co-ordination).

Among other things, the Federal Minister for Regional Planning, Building and Urban Development sponsors the following special activities :

- evaluation of information systems (working group W 52 of the CIB), Dr. Eisenblätter;

- classification SfB system (working group W 52 of the CIB), Prof. Sulzer;

- Performance Concept in Buildings (working group W 60 of the CIB and ISO/TC 59/SC 3), Standardization Committee on Building (NA-Bau in the DIN);

- participation in the preparation of European and international building regulations (CEB, CIB, ISO/TC 10, ISO/TC 98), Prof. Dr. König, Prof. Dr. Wesche;

- international co-ordination of structural engineering (regulations on reinforced concrete) (CEB, FIP, IVBH, ACI, RILEM), Prof. Dr. Kordina, Prof. Dr. Kupfer, Prof. Dr. Rüsch, Prof. Dr. Rehm, Prof. Dr. Weigler, Prof. Dr Leonhardt;

- participation in the UEAtc, Federal Institute for Material Testing, Dr. Jungbluth, Prof. Dr. Bornscheuer;

- development of a standardized modular and measurement co-ordination (ISO/TC 59), Standardization Committee on Building (NA-Bau in the DIN);

- participation in the technical committee (ISO/TC 163/heat insulation), NA-Bau in the DIN;

- collaboration in the international standardization work in the field of acoustics (ISO/TC 43/SC 2), Standardization Committee on Material Testing in the DIN;

- planning and building with regard to the climate (working group S4 of the CIB), Institute for Constructional Physics.

Furthermore, experts of the Federal Republic of Germany are working in various fields in panels that have not been enumerated here.

All of this enables us to approach our goal of an integrated research, a harmonization of individual national activities and interests in international panels, and of finding joint ways for future building. Public and other research bodies, research institutes and researchers on a voluntary basis should therefore show a similar co-operative attitude in regard to further research work for technical progress, for an increased productivity and for effective building, aspects which are focal points in the Federal Republic of Germany. By founding the Working Group on Building Research (Arbeitsgemeinschaft für Bauforschung (AGB)) incorporated in the Federal Ministry for Regional Planning, Building and Urban Development, it has been attempted to tackle common problems, to fix goals and priorities and to develop and overall strategy for the co-ordination of the activities in a clearing centre. The Federation has a great interest in all international level initiatives in this direction.

However, besides building research, the information flow, the information and documentation about findings in the field of building research should not be neglected. Lacking information hinders any innovation. In order to disseminate and exchange research results and in order to communicate effectively between research and application, we therefore think it necessary to intensify this transformation process by information and documentation systems. Experts should be oriented in time about intended, current and accomplished research projects. In the Federal Republic of Germany this orientation usually takes place by means of technical journals, series of publications, congresses, seminars and documentation centres. However, the information flow in this regard is not yet systematic. We would like to mention three publications that are favoured by the Federal Ministry for Regional Planning, Building and Urban Development (Bundesministerium für Raumordnung, Bauwesen und Städtebau, German abbreviation: BMBau): The "series of publications of the BMBau" ("Schriftenreihe des BMBau") (53 Bonn-Bad Godesberg), the "reports on building research" ("Berichte aus der Bauforschung") (Verlag Ernst & Sohn, Berlin (West)), and the "summaries on building research" ("Kurzberichte aus der Bauforschung") (Informationsverbundzentrum Bau & Raum, Stuttgart). Furthermore, there is the "bulletin of the Working Group on Building Research" ("Mitteilungsblatt der Arbeitsgemeinschaft für Bauforschung") (Bundesministerium für Raumordnung, Bauwesen und Städtebau, 53 Bonn-Bad Godesberg) which informs about intended, current and accomplished research projects. In addition, the Informationsverbundzentrum Raum & Bau in Stuttgart publishes a documentation about research reports – particularly from the Ministry for Regional Planning, Building and Urban Development – covering all fields of building, as well as regional planning and urban development. However, there is a great deal of information material. In order to attain to a systematic information from one source, the Working Group on Building Research (Arbeitsgemeinschaft für Bauforschung) has been founded some years ago. It operates as a voluntary organization into a working group of all bodies in the Federal Republic of Germany which promote research and provides information about national and increasingly about international research activities (for example, from Austria, Switzerland, Sweden, England, France). The registration of data in a data bank is intended. Other professional information systems, for example about building products, respectively, their standardization are being prepared with the aid of electronic data processing. However, they can only be fully effective if they do not only register and transfer national, but also international research activities in the most comprehensive way possible. This can only be possible within the framework of a special, international level information and documentation centre which co-ordinates the national activities. Experts of the Federal Republic of Germany take part in the present discussion of such an institution in the framework of the working group W 57 of the CIB (Informationsverbundzentrum Raum & Bau, Heinze Verlag).

Not only economical reasons speak in favour of such a documentation centre. Preconditions are a polyglot classification, standardized terms and a standardized size for the written information. Our country is very much interested in any development that helps to solve the problem of the registration and documentation of research results in a data bank, at least the results of the more advanced industrialized countries.

Netherlands

Contacts with R&D workers abroad are established in many different ways; for example through:

- journals or periodicals;
- exchange of staff and personnel, or other direct *ad hoc* contacts;
- work on international committees, etc.;
- projects financed by international organizations;
- R&D within the scope of institutions, or institutes, with international funding;
- international conferences, congresses, etc.

All these opportunities for international contacts obviously have intrinsic merits and demerits. The following measures are proposed in order to avoid or minimize inherent disadvantages:

The multiplicity of international organizations, governmental and non-governmental ones, calls for improved national coordination.

There is a tendency nowadays towards rather intensive international co-ordination of building regulations, specifications, etc. The result would be that the straightforward contribution of national building research institutions and institutes to national standardization and normalization lags behind in extent and speed. Accordingly attention should focus on the efficiency of international co-operation. Appropriate organizational steps should be taken and adequate funding evolved.

Participants in many congresses, and those in sessions of working parties, etc., often lose considerable time because of their host's organizing and financial problems (documents are distributed too late; there are no facilities for photocopying, etc., conference rooms which are not or hardly suitable; and so on).

It is, therefore, highly expedient for the various national governmental authorities to establish, for such occasions, a congress bureau which efficiently handles all pertinent matters of organization and solves any financial problems. The R&D people will then be in a position to devote time to their professional activities only.

Many international organizations could function and operate more effectively, if each is furnished with an adequately equipped central secretariat. National governmental authorities should, either through an agreed system of cost-sharing or through agreed distribution of tasks, provide for the central secretariat of the various professional organizations (CIB, CEB, CECM, ISO, CEN, FIP, RILEM, AIPC, etc.) concerned in order to safeguard the efficiency of the said contacts.

R&D activities and the reporting on them, both being of vital interest with a view to collaboration in international committees, often do not exactly fit the framework of R&D programmes in the co-operating institutions, etc. This may well mean that thus ensuing problems of capacity and financing seriously hamper the proper progress of the international work in question. It is therefore desirable to allow some scope, for the very purpose of international collaboration, in the R&D programmes concerned. As and when necessary, financial means should be earmarked for it.

Practically experienced R&D staff should from time to time review* appropriate international R&D activities in terms of recent past, present and future, along with obtained results.

---

* See, for example, Publication T 20 (1976) issued by the Swedish Council for Building Research: *Solar Energy Research in the USSR* (impressions from a study tour).